2018 PUNISHMENT CHART for North Carolina Crimes and Motor Vehicle Offenses

James M. Markham

UNC SCHOOL OF GOVERNMENT

The School of Government at the University of North Carolina at Chapel Hill works to improve the lives of North Carolinians by engaging in practical scholarship that helps public officials and citizens understand and improve state and local government. Established in 1931 as the Institute of Government, the School provides educational, advisory, and research services for state and local governments. The School of Government is also home to a nationally ranked Master of Public Administration program, the North Carolina Judicial College, and specialized centers focused on community and economic development, information technology, and environmental finance.

As the largest university-based local government training, advisory, and research organization in the United States, the School of Government offers up to 200 courses, webinars, and specialized conferences for more than 12,000 public officials each year. In addition, faculty members annually publish approximately 50 books, manuals, reports, articles, bulletins, and other print and online content related to state and local government. The School also produces the *Daily Bulletin Online* each day the General Assembly is in session, reporting on activities for members of the legislature and others who need to follow the course of legislation.

Operating support for the School of Government's programs and activities comes from many sources, including state appropriations, local government membership dues, private contributions, publication sales, course fees, and service contracts.

Visit sog.unc.edu or call 919.966.5381 for more information on the School's courses, publications, programs, and services.

Printed in the United States of America

30 29 28 27 26 2 3 4 5 6

ISBN 978-1-56011-945-6

Contents

Preface

This publication replaces the 2015 edition, written by former School of Government faculty member Bob Farb. This edition is current through 2018.

When the punishment for an offense listed in this publication is set out in another statute, that statutory citation is listed after the statutory citation for the offense. Pertinent changes in statutory offenses made between the 2015 legislative session and November 1, 2018, are noted in the footnotes. For changes that may have occurred before then, the reader should review prior punishment charts or the general statute's history and editor's notes. All previous editions of this publication are available online at bit.ly/punishmentcharts.

Offenses subject to the Crime Victims' Rights Act (G.S. 15A-830 through G.S. 15A-841) are listed in Appendix A. That list is likely to expand pursuant to a constitutional amendment approved by the voters of North Carolina in November 2018, effective August 31, 2019 (S.L. 2018-110).

Offenses that require registration as a sex offender are noted in the footnotes throughout the text and collected in Appendix B.

Offenses that trigger a driver's license revocation are noted in the footnotes and collected in Appendix C. School of Government faculty member Shea Denning authored the contents of that appendix.

This book focuses on the criminal punishment associated with various offenses in North Carolina, but equally important (and sometimes more important) for many defendants will be the collateral consequences of the conviction. Two resources from the School of Government, both created by School faculty member John Rubin, are available to help lawyers, court officials, and citizens navigate that complicated area of law.

- Relief from a Criminal Conviction: A Digital Guide to Expunctions, Certificates of Relief, and Other Procedures in North Carolina (2017), www.sog.unc.edu/resources/microsites/relief-criminal-conviction
- Collateral Consequences Assessment Tool (C-CAT), ccat.sog.unc.edu

I thank Shea Denning, John Rubin, and Bob Farb for their contributions to this publication. I am also grateful to Leslie Watkins, Jennifer Henderson, Dan Soileau, and Kevin Justice for their work editing and publishing the book. Any mistakes that remain are my own.

Jamie Markham
Chapel Hill
November 2018

MINIMUM

Felony Offenses Committed on or after **October 1, 2013**

MINIMUM SENTENCES AND DISPOSITIONAL OPTIONS

OFFENSE CLASS	PRIOR RECORD LEVEL I 0–1 Pt	II 2–5 Pts	III 6–9 Pts	IV 10–13 Pts	V 14–17 Pts	VI 18+ Pts	
A Max. Death or Life w/o Parole	Death or Life without Parole Defendant under 18 at Time of Offense: Life with or without Parole						
B1 Max. Life w/o Parole	A	A	A	A	A	A	**DISPOSITION**
	240–300	276–345	317–397	365–456	Life w/o Parole	Life w/o Parole	Aggravated
	192–240	**221–276**	**254–317**	**292–365**	**336–420**	**386–483**	**PRESUMPTIVE**
	144–192	166–221	190–254	219–292	252–336	290–386	Mitigated
B2 Max. 484 (*532*)	A (EM)	A (EM)	A	A	A	A	
	157–196	180–225	207–258	238–297	273–342	314–393	
	125–157	**144–180**	**165–207**	**190–238**	**219–273**	**251–314**	
	94–125	108–144	124–165	143–190	164–219	189–251	
C Max. 231 (*279*)	A (EM)	A (EM)	A	A	A	A	
	73–92	83–104	96–120	110–138	127–159	146–182	
	58–73	**67–83**	**77–96**	**88–110**	**101–127**	**117–146**	
	44–58	50–67	58–77	66–88	76–101	87–117	
D Max. 204 (*252*)	A (EM)	A (EM)	A	A	A	A	
	64–80	73–92	84–105	97–121	111–139	128–160	
	51–64	**59–73**	**67–84**	**78–97**	**89–111**	**103–128**	
	ASR 38–51	ASR 44–59	ASR 51–67	58–78	67–89	77–103	
E Max. 88 (*136*)	I/A	I/A	A	A	A	A	
	25–31	29–36	33–41	38–48	44–55	50–63	
	20–25	**23–29**	**26–33**	**30–38**	**35–44**	**40–50**	
	ASR 15–20	ASR 17–23	ASR 20–26	ASR 23–30	26–35	30–40	
F Max. 59	I/A	I/A	I/A	A	A	A	
	16–20	19–23	21–27	25–31	28–36	33–41	
	13–16	**15–19**	**17–21**	**20–25**	**23–28**	**26–33**	
	ASR 10–13	ASR 11–15	ASR 13–17	ASR 15–20	ASR 17–23	20–26	
G Max. 47	I/A	I/A	I/A	I/A	A	A	
	13–16	14–18	17–21	19–24	22–27	25–31	
	10–13	**12–14**	**13–17**	**15–19**	**17–22**	**20–25**	
	ASR 8–10	ASR 9–12	ASR 10–13	ASR 11–15	ASR 13–17	ASR 15–20	
H Max. 39	C/I/A	I/A	I/A	I/A	I/A	A	
	6–8	8–10	10–12	11–14	15–19	20–25	
	5–6	**6–8**	**8–10**	**9–11**	**12–15**	**16–20**	
	ASR 4–5	ASR 4–6	ASR 6–8	ASR 7–9	ASR 9–12	ASR 12–16	
I Max. 24	C	C/I	I	I/A	I/A	I/A	
	6–8	6–8	6–8	8–10	9–11	10–12	
	4–6	**4–6**	**5–6**	**6–8**	**7–9**	**8–10**	
	3–4	3–4	4–5	4–6	5–7	6–8	

Note: Numbers shown are in months. The number shown below each offense class reflects the maximum possible sentence for that class of offense (the highest maximum sentence from the aggravated range in prior record level VI). The maximum sentence for a defendant convicted of a reportable Class B1 through E sex crime is indicated in parentheses.

A—Active Punishment
I—Intermediate Punishment
C—Community Punishment

EM **Extraordinary Mitigation** (possible eligibility).

ASR **Advanced Supervised Release** (possible eligibility).

MAXIMUM SENTENCES

The tables below show the maximum sentence that corresponds to each minimum sentence. For minimum sentences of 340 months or more, the maximum sentence is 120 percent of the minimum sentence, rounded to the next highest month, plus 12 additional months. G.S. 15A-1340.17(e1).

Sex Crimes: The maximum sentence for a Class B1 through E felony subject to the registration requirements of G.S. Chapter 14, Article 27A is 120 percent of the minimum sentence, rounded to the next highest month, plus 60 additional months, as indicated in parentheses below. G.S. 15A-1340.17(f).

FOR OFFENSE CLASSES B1 THROUGH E [Minimum Sentence → Corresponding Maximum (*Sex Crimes*)]

15 → 30 (78)	56 → 80 (128)	97 → 129 (177)	138 → 178 (226)	179 → 227 (275)	220 → 276 (324)	261 → 326 (374)	302 → 375 (423)
16 → 32 (80)	57 → 81 (129)	98 → 130 (178)	139 → 179 (227)	180 → 228 (276)	221 → 278 (326)	262 → 327 (375)	303 → 376 (424)
17 → 33 (81)	58 → 82 (130)	99 → 131 (179)	140 → 180 (228)	181 → 230 (278)	222 → 279 (327)	263 → 328 (376)	304 → 377 (425)
18 → 34 (82)	59 → 83 (131)	100 → 132 (180)	141 → 182 (230)	182 → 231 (279)	223 → 280 (328)	264 → 329 (377)	305 → 378 (426)
19 → 35 (83)	60 → 84 (132)	101 → 134 (182)	142 → 183 (231)	183 → 232 (280)	224 → 281 (329)	265 → 330 (378)	306 → 380 (428)
20 → 36 (84)	61 → 86 (134)	102 → 135 (183)	143 → 184 (232)	184 → 233 (281)	225 → 282 (330)	266 → 332 (380)	307 → 381 (429)
21 → 38 (86)	62 → 87 (135)	103 → 136 (184)	144 → 185 (233)	185 → 234 (282)	226 → 284 (332)	267 → 333 (381)	308 → 382 (430)
22 → 39 (87)	63 → 88 (136)	104 → 137 (185)	145 → 186 (234)	186 → 236 (284)	227 → 285 (333)	268 → 334 (382)	309 → 383 (431)
23 → 40 (88)	64 → 89 (137)	105 → 138 (186)	146 → 188 (236)	187 → 237 (285)	228 → 286 (334)	269 → 335 (383)	310 → 384 (432)
24 → 41 (89)	65 → 90 (138)	106 → 140 (188)	147 → 189 (237)	188 → 238 (286)	229 → 287 (335)	270 → 336 (384)	311 → 386 (434)
25 → 42 (90)	66 → 92 (140)	107 → 141 (189)	148 → 190 (238)	189 → 239 (287)	230 → 288 (336)	271 → 338 (386)	312 → 387 (435)
26 → 44 (92)	67 → 93 (141)	108 → 142 (190)	149 → 191 (239)	190 → 240 (288)	231 → 290 (338)	272 → 339 (387)	313 → 388 (436)
27 → 45 (93)	68 → 94 (142)	109 → 143 (191)	150 → 192 (240)	191 → 242 (290)	232 → 291 (339)	273 → 340 (388)	314 → 389 (437)
28 → 46 (94)	69 → 95 (143)	110 → 144 (192)	151 → 194 (242)	192 → 243 (291)	233 → 292 (340)	274 → 341 (389)	315 → 390 (438)
29 → 47 (95)	70 → 96 (144)	111 → 146 (194)	152 → 195 (243)	193 → 244 (292)	234 → 293 (341)	275 → 342 (390)	316 → 392 (440)
30 → 48 (96)	71 → 98 (146)	112 → 147 (195)	153 → 196 (244)	194 → 245 (293)	235 → 294 (342)	276 → 344 (392)	317 → 393 (441)
31 → 50 (98)	72 → 99 (147)	113 → 148 (196)	154 → 197 (245)	195 → 246 (294)	236 → 296 (344)	277 → 345 (393)	318 → 394 (442)
32 → 51 (99)	73 → 100 (148)	114 → 149 (197)	155 → 198 (246)	196 → 248 (296)	237 → 297 (345)	278 → 346 (394)	319 → 395 (443)
33 → 52 (100)	74 → 101 (149)	115 → 150 (198)	156 → 200 (248)	197 → 249 (297)	238 → 298 (346)	279 → 347 (395)	320 → 396 (444)
34 → 53 (101)	75 → 102 (150)	116 → 152 (200)	157 → 201 (249)	198 → 250 (298)	239 → 299 (347)	280 → 348 (396)	321 → 398 (446)
35 → 54 (102)	76 → 104 (152)	117 → 153 (201)	158 → 202 (250)	199 → 251 (299)	240 → 300 (348)	281 → 350 (398)	322 → 399 (447)
36 → 56 (104)	77 → 105 (153)	118 → 154 (202)	159 → 203 (251)	200 → 252 (300)	241 → 302 (350)	282 → 351 (399)	323 → 400 (448)
37 → 57 (105)	78 → 106 (154)	119 → 155 (203)	160 → 204 (252)	201 → 254 (302)	242 → 303 (351)	283 → 352 (400)	324 → 401 (449)
38 → 58 (106)	79 → 107 (155)	120 → 156 (204)	161 → 206 (254)	202 → 255 (303)	243 → 304 (352)	284 → 353 (401)	325 → 402 (450)
39 → 59 (107)	80 → 108 (156)	121 → 158 (206)	162 → 207 (255)	203 → 256 (304)	244 → 305 (353)	285 → 354 (402)	326 → 404 (452)
40 → 60 (108)	81 → 110 (158)	122 → 159 (207)	163 → 208 (256)	204 → 257 (305)	245 → 306 (354)	286 → 356 (404)	327 → 405 (453)
41 → 62 (110)	82 → 111 (159)	123 → 160 (208)	164 → 209 (257)	205 → 258 (306)	246 → 308 (356)	287 → 357 (405)	328 → 406 (454)
42 → 63 (111)	83 → 112 (160)	124 → 161 (209)	165 → 210 (258)	206 → 260 (308)	247 → 309 (357)	288 → 358 (406)	329 → 407 (455)
43 → 64 (112)	84 → 113 (161)	125 → 162 (210)	166 → 212 (260)	207 → 261 (309)	248 → 310 (358)	289 → 359 (407)	330 → 408 (456)
44 → 65 (113)	85 → 114 (162)	126 → 164 (212)	167 → 213 (261)	208 → 262 (310)	249 → 311 (359)	290 → 360 (408)	331 → 410 (458)
45 → 66 (114)	86 → 116 (164)	127 → 165 (213)	168 → 214 (262)	209 → 263 (311)	250 → 312 (360)	291 → 362 (410)	332 → 411 (459)
46 → 68 (116)	87 → 117 (165)	128 → 166 (214)	169 → 215 (263)	210 → 264 (312)	251 → 314 (362)	292 → 363 (411)	333 → 412 (460)
47 → 69 (117)	88 → 118 (166)	129 → 167 (215)	170 → 216 (264)	211 → 266 (314)	252 → 315 (363)	293 → 364 (412)	334 → 413 (461)
48 → 70 (118)	89 → 119 (167)	130 → 168 (216)	171 → 218 (266)	212 → 267 (315)	253 → 316 (364)	294 → 365 (413)	335 → 414 (462)
49 → 71 (119)	90 → 120 (168)	131 → 170 (218)	172 → 219 (267)	213 → 268 (316)	254 → 317 (365)	295 → 366 (414)	336 → 416 (464)
50 → 72 (120)	91 → 122 (170)	132 → 171 (219)	173 → 220 (268)	214 → 269 (317)	255 → 318 (366)	296 → 368 (416)	337 → 417 (465)
51 → 74 (122)	92 → 123 (171)	133 → 172 (220)	174 → 221 (269)	215 → 270 (318)	256 → 320 (368)	297 → 369 (417)	338 → 418 (466)
52 → 75 (123)	93 → 124 (172)	134 → 173 (221)	175 → 222 (270)	216 → 272 (320)	257 → 321 (369)	298 → 370 (418)	339 → 419 (467)
53 → 76 (124)	94 → 125 (173)	135 → 174 (222)	176 → 224 (272)	217 → 273 (321)	258 → 322 (370)	299 → 371 (419)	
54 → 77 (125)	95 → 126 (174)	136 → 176 (224)	177 → 225 (273)	218 → 274 (322)	259 → 323 (371)	300 → 372 (420)	
55 → 78 (126)	96 → 128 (176)	137 → 177 (225)	178 → 226 (274)	219 → 275 (323)	260 → 324 (372)	301 → 374 (422)	

FOR OFFENSE CLASSES F THROUGH I [Minimum Sentence → Corresponding Maximum]

3 → 13	9 → 20	15 → 27	21 → 35	27 → 42	33 → 49	39 → 56	45 → 63
4 → 14	10 → 21	16 → 29	22 → 36	28 → 43	34 → 50	40 → 57	46 → 65
5 → 15	11 → 23	17 → 30	23 → 37	29 → 44	35 → 51	41 → 59	47 → 66
6 → 17	12 → 24	18 → 31	24 → 38	30 → 45	36 → 53	42 → 60	48 → 67
7 → 18	13 → 25	19 → 32	25 → 39	31 → 47	37 → 54	43 → 61	49 → 68
8 → 19	14 → 26	20 → 33	26 → 41	32 → 48	38 → 55	44 → 62	

Length of Probation Period

The original period of probation for a felony sentenced under Structured Sentencing must fall within the following limits:

- Community—12 to 30 months
- Intermediate—18 to 36 months

The court may depart from those ranges with a finding that a longer or shorter period is required. The maximum permissible period with a finding is 5 years. G.S. 15A-1343.2.

Post-Release Supervision

Class F–I felony—9 months
Class B1–E felony—12 months
Crimes requiring sex offender registration—5 years

Fines

Any felony sentence may include a fine. Unless otherwise provided for a specific offense, the amount of the fine is in the discretion of the court. G.S. 15A-1340.17(b).

Punishment for Covered Driving While Impaired (DWI) Offenses Committed on or after **October 1, 2013**

Punishment Level Controlling Statute *Factors*	**Imprisonment and Mandatory Probation Conditions**	**Fine**
Aggravated Level One G.S. 20-179(f3) *Three or more grossly aggravating factors*	• 12 months minimum to 36 months maximum • If suspended – Imprisonment of at least 120 days as a condition of special probation – Requirement that defendant abstain from alcohol consumption for a minimum of 120 days to a maximum of the term of probation, as verified by continuous alcohol monitoring (CAM) system – Requirement that defendant obtain a substance abuse assessment and education or treatment required by G.S. 20-17.6	Up to $10,000
Level One G.S. 20-179(g) *Grossly aggravating factor in G.S. 20-179(c)(4) or two other grossly aggravating factors*	• 30 days minimum to 24 months maximum • If suspended – Special probation requiring (1) imprisonment of at least 30 days or (2) imprisonment of at least 10 days and alcohol abstinence and CAM for at least 120 days – Requirement that defendant obtain a substance abuse assessment and education or treatment required by G.S. 20-17.6	Up to $4,000
Level Two G.S. 20-179(h) *One grossly aggravating factor, other than the grossly aggravating factor in G.S. 20-179(c)(4)*	• 7 days minimum to 12 months maximum • If suspended – Special probation requiring (1) imprisonment of at least 7 days or (2) alcohol abstinence and CAM for at least 90 days ○ If Level Two based on prior conviction or DWLR for an impaired driving revocation and prior conviction occurred within five years, sentence must require 240 hours of community service if no imprisonment imposed – Requirement that defendant obtain a substance abuse assessment and education or treatment required by G.S. 20-17.6	Up to $2,000
Level Three G.S. 20-179(i) *Aggravating factors substantially outweigh any mitigating factors*	• 72 hours minimum to 6 months maximum • If suspended – Must require one or both of the following ○ Imprisonment for at least 72 hours as a condition of special probation ○ Community service for a term of at least 72 hours – Requirement that defendant obtain a substance abuse assessment and education or treatment required by G.S. 20-17.6	Up to $1,000
Level Four G.S. 20-179(j) *No aggravating and mitigating factors or aggravating factors are substantially counterbalanced by mitigating factors*	• 48 hours minimum to 120 days maximum • If suspended – Must require one or both of the following ○ Imprisonment for 48 hours as a condition of special probation ○ Community service for a term of 48 hours – Requirement that defendant obtain a substance abuse assessment and education or treatment required by G.S. 20-17.6	Up to $500
Level Five G.S. 20-179(k) *Mitigating factors substantially outweigh aggravating factors*	• 24 hours minimum to 60 days maximum • If suspended – Must require one or both of the following ○ Imprisonment for 24 hours as a condition of special probation ○ Community service for a term of 24 hours – Requirement that defendant obtain a substance abuse assessment and education or treatment required by G.S. 20-17.6	Up to $200

Drug Trafficking Sentencing (G.S. 90-95(h))

Drug trafficking is not sentenced using the regular Structured Sentencing grid. Instead, a person convicted of drug trafficking must be sentenced as set out below, including the mandatory fine, regardless of his or her prior criminal record.

Offense Class and Minimum Fines for Drug Trafficking

Drug	Amount	Class	Fine (not less than)
Marijuana	In excess of 10 lbs.–49 lbs.	H	$ 5,000
	50–1,999 lbs.	G	$ 25,000
	2,000–9,999	F	$ 50,000
	10,000 or more	D	$200,000
Methaqualone	1,000–4,999 dosage units	G	$ 25,000
	5,000–9,999	F	$ 50,000
	10,000 or more	D	$200,000
Cocaine	28–199 grams	G	$ 50,000
	200–399	F	$100,000
	400 or more	D	$250,000
Methamphetamine	28–199 grams	F	$ 50,000
	200–399	E	$100,000
	400 or more	C	$250,000
Amphetamine	28–199 grams	H	$ 5,000
	200–399	G	$ 25,000
	400 or more	E	$100,000
Opium, Opiate, Opioid, or Heroin*	4–13 grams	F	$ 50,000
	14–27	E	$100,000
	28 or more	C	$500,000
LSD	100–499 units	G	$ 25,000
	500–999	F	$ 50,000
	1,000 or more	D	$200,000
MDA/MDMA	100–499 units/28–199 grams	G	$ 25,000
	500–999 units/200–399 grams	F	$ 50,000
	1,000 units/400 grams or more	D	$250,000
Substituted Cathinones*	28–199 grams	F	$ 50,000
	200–399	E	$100,000
	400 or more	C	$250,000
Synthetic Cannabinoids	In excess of 50–249 dosage units**	H	$ 5,000
	250–1,249	G	$ 25,000
	1,250–3,749	F	$ 50,000
	3,750 or more	D	$200,000

* Effective December 1, 2018. S.L. 2018-44.

**A "dosage unit" is 3 grams of synthetic cannabinoid or any mixture containing such substance.

Minimum-Maximum Sentences for Drug Trafficking Crimes, by Offense Class

	Offense Committed **On/After** 12/1/2012		Offense Committed **Before** 12/1/2012	
Class	Minimum	Maximum	Minimum	Maximum
Class C	225 mos.	282	225 mos.	279
Class D	175	222	175	219
Class E	90	120	90	117
Class F	70	93	70	84
Class G	35	51	35	42
Class H	25	39	25	30

Misdemeanor Offenses Committed on or after **December 1, 2013**

<table>
<tr><th rowspan="2">OFFENSE CLASS</th><th colspan="4">PRIOR CONVICTION LEVEL</th></tr>
<tr><th>I
No Prior Convictions</th><th colspan="2">II
One to Four Prior Convictions</th><th>III
Five or More Prior Convictions</th></tr>
<tr><td rowspan="2">A1</td><td>C/I/A</td><td colspan="2">C/I/A</td><td>C/I/A</td></tr>
<tr><td>1–60 days</td><td colspan="2">1–75 days</td><td>1–150 days</td></tr>
<tr><td rowspan="2">1</td><td>C</td><td colspan="2">C/I/A</td><td>C/I/A</td></tr>
<tr><td>1–45 days</td><td colspan="2">1–45 days</td><td>1–120 days</td></tr>
<tr><td rowspan="2">2</td><td>C</td><td colspan="2">C/I</td><td>C/I/A</td></tr>
<tr><td>1–30 days</td><td colspan="2">1–45 days</td><td>1–60 days</td></tr>
<tr><td></td><td></td><td>One to Three Prior Convictions</td><td>Four Prior Convictions</td><td></td></tr>
<tr><td rowspan="2">3</td><td>C</td><td>C</td><td>C/I</td><td>C/I/A</td></tr>
<tr><td>Fine Only*
1–10 days</td><td>Fine Only*
1–15 days</td><td>1–15 days</td><td>1–20 days</td></tr>
</table>

*Unless otherwise provided for a specific offense, the judgment for a person convicted of a Class 3 misdemeanor who has no more than three prior convictions shall consist only of a fine.

A—Active Punishment **I**—Intermediate Punishment **C**—Community Punishment

Length of Probation Period

The original period of probation for a misdemeanor sentenced under Structured Sentencing must fall within the following limits:

- Community—6 to 18 months
- Intermediate—12 to 24 months

The court may depart from those ranges with a finding that a longer or shorter period is required. The maximum permissible period with a finding is 5 years. G.S. 15A-1343.2.

Fines

Any misdemeanor sentence may include a fine. Unless otherwise provided for a specific offense, the maximum fine for a misdemeanor is as follows:

- Class A1—Court discretion
- Class 1—Court discretion
- Class 2—$1,000
- Class 3—$200

Local ordinance violation: $50, unless the ordinance provides for a larger amount, up to $500. G.S. 15A-1340.23(b); 14-4.

2018 Punishment Chart for North Carolina Crimes and Motor Vehicle Offenses

Statute	Description of Offense	Punishment
Chapter 5A: Contempt[1]		
5A-11(a), -12(a)	Criminal contempt, generally	Censure, imprisonment up to 30 days, fine up to $500, or combination thereof[2]
5A-11(a)(8), -12(a)(1)	Criminal contempt by willful refusal to testify after being granted immunity	Censure, imprisonment up to six months, fine up to $500, or combination thereof
5A-11(a)(9a), -12(a)	Criminal contempt by willful refusal to comply with condition of probation	Censure, imprisonment up to 30 days, fine up to $500, or combination thereof[3]
5A-11(a)(9b), -12(a)	Criminal contempt by willful refusal to accept or to comply with post-release supervision by defendant subject to sex offender registration requirements	Censure, imprisonment up to 30 days, fine up to $500, or combination thereof
5A-12(a)(2)	Criminal contempt by failure to comply with nontestimonial identification order	Censure, imprisonment up to 90 days, fine up to $500, or combination thereof
5A-12(a)(3)	Criminal contempt by failure to comply with order to pay child support	Censure, imprisonment up to 30 days, fine up to $500, or combination thereof[4]

---

1. Although criminal contempt is characterized as a crime, an adjudication of criminal contempt that is punishable by a maximum of 30 days' imprisonment does not constitute a prior conviction for purposes of structured sentencing. *See* State v. Reaves, 142 N.C. App. 629 (2001) (court so holds but declines to decide whether adjudication of criminal contempt with greater maximum punishment constitutes prior conviction). The court may run sentences for multiple criminal contempt findings consecutively, State v. Burrow, ___ N.C. App. ___, 789 S.E.2d 923 (2016); however, a total consecutive sentence exceeding 180 days could trigger a defendant's Sixth Amendment right to a jury trial, *see* Codispoti v. Pennsylvania, 418 U.S. 506 (1974).

2. G.S. 5A-12(c) authorizes the judge to reduce or withdraw the sentence imposed at any time "if warranted by the conduct of the contemnor and the ends of justice." G.S. 5A-12(d) states that a person may not be held in both criminal and civil contempt for the same conduct.

3. A revoked probationer is entitled to credit for time served for contempt under G.S. 15A-1344(e1) and G.S. 15-196.1. State v. Belcher, 173 N.C. App. 620 (2005). G.S. 15A-1368.2(b) provides, however, that a defendant punished for criminal contempt for refusing post-release supervision is not eligible for credit for time served.

4. G.S. 5A-12(a)(3) authorizes imprisonment up to 120 days for a single act of criminal contempt resulting from the failure to pay child support, provided the sentence is suspended for conditions reasonably related to the contemnor's payment of child support.

Statute	Description of Offense	Punishment

Chapter 7B: Juvenile Code

7B-301(b)	Failing to report abuse, neglect, dependency, or death due to maltreatment of juvenile as required by 7B-301(a) or preventing another from making report	Class 1 misdemeanor
7B-301(c)	Director of social services receives report of sexual abuse of juvenile in child care facility and fails to notify State Bureau of Investigation of report as required by 7B-301(a)	Class 1 misdemeanor

Chapter 14: Criminal Law

Article 1: Felonies and Misdemeanors[5]

14-2.4(a)	Conspiracy to commit felony	Unless different classification stated, punishable one class lower than felony defendant conspired to commit[6]
14-2.4(b)	Conspiracy to commit misdemeanor	Unless different classification stated, punishable one class lower than misdemeanor defendant conspired to commit[7]
14-2.5	Attempt to commit felony or misdemeanor	Unless different classification stated, punishable one class lower than offense attempted[8]
14-2.6(a)	Solicitation to commit felony	Unless different classification stated, punishable two classes lower than felony solicited[9]

5. Property acquired as a result of a felony other than a nonwillful homicide is subject to forfeiture as provided in G.S. 14-2.3.

6. Unless a different classification is stated, conspiracy to commit a Class A or B1 felony is a Class B2 felony, conspiracy to commit a Class B2 felony is a Class C felony, and conspiracy to commit a Class I felony is a Class 1 misdemeanor. G.S. 14-2.4(a).

7. Unless a different classification is stated, conspiracy to commit a Class 3 misdemeanor is a Class 3 misdemeanor. G.S. 14-2.4(b).

8. Unless a different classification is stated, attempt to commit a Class A or B1 felony is a Class B2 felony, attempt to commit a Class B2 felony is a Class C felony, attempt to commit a Class I felony is a Class 1 misdemeanor, and attempt to commit a Class 3 misdemeanor is a Class 3 misdemeanor. *See* G.S. 14-2.5.

9. Unless a different classification is stated, solicitation to commit a Class A or B1 felony is a Class C felony, solicitation to commit a Class B2 felony is a Class D felony, solicitation to commit a Class H felony is a Class 1 misdemeanor, and solicitation to commit a Class I felony is a Class 2 misdemeanor. *See* G.S. 14-2.6(a).

Statute	Description of Offense	Punishment
14-2.6(b)	Solicitation to commit misdemeanor	Unless different classification stated, punishable as Class 3 misdemeanor[10]
14-3(a)	Misdemeanors without a specific classification and punishment	Class 1 misdemeanor[11]
14-3(b)	Misdemeanors that are infamous, done in secrecy and malice, or committed with deceit and intent to defraud	If no specific punishment prescribed, punishable as Class H felony[12]
14-3(c)	Misdemeanors committed because of the victim's race, color, religion, nationality, or country of origin	Class 2 or 3 misdemeanor committed for proscribed reason punishable as Class 1 misdemeanor; Class A1 or 1 misdemeanor committed for proscribed reason punishable as Class H felony
14-4(a)	Violation of local ordinance, except those in 14-4(b)	Class 3 misdemeanor[13]
14-4(b)	Violation of local ordinance regulating operation or parking of vehicles	Infraction with maximum $50 penalty

Article 2: Principals and Accessories

14-5.2	Accessory before the fact to felony	Punishable as principal[14]

10. Although G.S. 14-2.6 establishes the punishment for soliciting another to commit a misdemeanor, North Carolina law may only recognize as a criminal offense solicitation to commit certain misdemeanors.

11. Misdemeanors with specific punishments but without specific classifications are classified as follows: (1) as Class 1 misdemeanors if punishable by more than six months' imprisonment; (2) as Class 2 misdemeanors if punishable by more than 30 days but not more than six months' imprisonment; and (3) as Class 3 misdemeanors if punishable by imprisonment of 30 days or less or by a fine only. *See* G.S. 14-3(a).

12. A misdemeanor may not be elevated to a felony under this statute unless the indictment specifically alleges that the offense was infamous, done in secrecy or malice, or done with deceit and intent to defraud.

13. G.S. 14-4(a) allows a fine of up to $500 for a violation if the ordinance so provides. If the ordinance does not expressly provide for a fine greater than $50, the fine may not exceed $50.

14. In 1981 the General Assembly abolished the distinction between accessories before the fact and principals in the commission of felonies. Under G.S. 14-5.2, defendants who would have been guilty of accessory before the fact under former law are now punished as principals. G.S. 14-5.2 creates one exception to this rule: If a person who would have been convicted of accessory before the fact under former law is convicted of a capital offense, and the conviction is based solely on the uncorroborated testimony of one or more principals, co-conspirators, or accessories to the crime, the defendant is guilty of a Class B2 felony. Even if this exception is not applicable, it would be unconstitutional in certain circumstances to impose the death penalty on a defendant who might otherwise be an accessory before the fact to a capital offense. *See* Tison v. Arizona, 481 U.S. 137 (1987); Enmund v. Florida, 458 U.S. 782 (1982); N.C. Pattern Jury Instruction 150.10.

This distinction is not made between principals and accessories before the fact concerning misdemeanors. Unless otherwise provided, defendants who participate in misdemeanors "are indictable and punishable as principals." State v. Bennett, 237 N.C. 749, 752 (1953).

Statute	Description of Offense	Punishment
14-7	Accessory after the fact to felony	Unless different classification stated, punishable two classes lower than felony committed by principal[15]
Article 2A: Habitual Felons		
14-7.1 through -7.6	Habitual felon	Punishable four classes higher than felony for which person was convicted; mandatory consecutive sentence[16]
Article 2B: Violent Habitual Felons		
14-7.7 through -7.12	Violent habitual felon	Life imprisonment without parole; mandatory consecutive sentence[17]
Article 2C: Continuing Criminal Enterprise		
14-7.20(a)	Continuing criminal enterprise	Class H felony[18]
14-7.20(a1)	Continuing criminal enterprise when underlying felony is terrorism	Class D felony[19]

15. Unless a different classification is stated, accessory after the fact to a Class A or B1 felony is a Class C felony, accessory after the fact to a Class B2 felony is a Class D felony, accessory after the fact to a Class H felony is a Class 1 misdemeanor, and accessory after the fact to a Class I felony is a Class 2 misdemeanor. *See* G.S. 14-7.

A participant in a crime cannot be an accessory after the fact to that crime. *See* State v. McIntosh, 260 N.C. 749 (1963). In the absence of a statute providing otherwise, a person apparently may not be convicted of being an accessory after the fact to a misdemeanor.

16. Being a habitual felon is not a crime. It is a status that subjects the defendant to an enhanced punishment upon conviction of a felony after having been convicted of three prior felonies. For principal felonies committed before December 1, 2011, a habitual felon is sentenced as a Class C felon for the underlying felony (except if the conviction was for a Class A, B1, or B2 felony). Effective for principal felonies committed on or after December 1, 2011, the sentence is four classes higher than the underlying felony (except when the conviction is for a Class A, B1, or B2 felony) but never higher than a Class C felony. The sentence must run consecutively with and must begin to run at the expiration of any sentence being served by the person at the time of sentencing. When two or more offenses are being disposed of in the same proceeding, however, the court is not required to impose consecutive sentences. State v. Haymond, 203 N.C. App. 151 (2010).

17. Being a violent habitual felon is not a crime. It is a status that subjects the defendant to an enhanced punishment upon conviction of a third "violent felony" as defined in G.S. 14-7.7. Upon conviction as a violent habitual felon, the defendant must be sentenced to life imprisonment without parole, except when the death penalty is imposed. A suspended sentence or probation is not allowed. The sentence must run consecutively with and must begin to run at the expiration of any sentence being served by the person at the time of sentencing. When two or more offenses are being disposed of in the same proceeding, however, the court is not required to impose consecutive sentences. *Cf.* State v. Haymond, 203 N.C. App. 151 (2010).

18. G.S. 14-7.20(b) provides that a person convicted of engaging in a continuing criminal enterprise forfeits to the state his or her profits from and interest in the enterprise.

19. G.S. 14-7.20(b) provides that a person convicted of engaging in a continuing criminal enterprise forfeits to the state his or her profits from and interest in the enterprise.

Statute	Description of Offense	Punishment
Article 2D: Habitual Breaking and Entering		
14-7.25 through -7.31	Habitual breaking and entering	Class E felony; mandatory consecutive sentence[20]
Article 2E: Armed Habitual Felon		
14-7.35 through -7.41	Armed habitual felon	Class C felony; minimum sentence of at least 120 months; mandatory consecutive sentence[21]
Article 3A: Terrorism		
14-10.1	Terrorism	Felony one class higher than offense that is underlying act of violence[22]
Article 4A: Prohibited Secret Societies and Activities		
14-12.12(a), -12.15	Placing burning cross on property of another without consent	Class 1 misdemeanor
14-12.12(b), -12.15	Placing burning cross on property of another or on public street, highway, or place with intent to intimidate, prevent lawful act, or cause unlawful act	Class H felony
14-12.13, -12.15	Placing exhibit in any location with intent to intimidate, prevent lawful act, or cause unlawful act	Class H felony
14-12.14, -12.15	Wearing mask, hood, or other disguise while placing exhibit in any location with intent to intimidate, prevent lawful act, or cause unlawful act	Class H felony

20. Habitual breaking and entering is a status, not a crime. Legislation enacted in 2011 established this status, effective for a principal felony of "breaking and entering," as defined in G.S. 14-7.25, that was committed on or after December 1, 2011. A defendant who commits the principal felony after attaining the status is sentenced as a Class E felon. The sentence must run consecutively with and commence at the expiration of any sentence being served by the defendant. A conviction used to establish the status cannot be used to determine the defendant's prior record level. When two or more offenses are being disposed of in the same proceeding, however, the court is not required to impose consecutive sentences. *Cf.* State v. Haymond, 203 N.C. App. 151 (2010).

21. Being an armed habitual felon is not a crime. It is a status that subjects the defendant to an enhanced punishment for a conviction of a firearm-related felony as defined in G.S. 14-7.35(2). A defendant is sentenced for the substantive felony as a Class C felon except when the felon has been sentenced as a Class A, B1, or B2 felon. The sentence must run consecutively with and commence at the expiration of any sentence being served by the defendant. When two or more offenses are being disposed of in the same proceeding, however, the court is not required to impose consecutive sentences. *Cf.* State v. Haymond, 203 N.C. App. 151 (2010). A suspended sentence or probation is not allowed. A sentence may not also be enhanced under G.S. 15A-1340.16A (enhanced sentence for using firearm or deadly weapon during felony).

22. If the underlying act of violence is a Class A or B1 felony, then a violation of this statute is a Class B1 felony.

Statute	Description of Offense	Punishment
Article 5: Counterfeiting and Issuing Monetary Substitutes		
14-13	Counterfeiting coin or uttering counterfeit coin	Class I felony
14-14	Possession of tools for counterfeiting coin	Class I felony
Article 5A: Endangering Executive, Legislative, and Court Officers		
14-16.6(a)	Assault on officer or attack on officer's residence, office, or means of transport	Class I felony
14-16.6(b)	Violation of 14-16.6(a) with deadly weapon	Class F felony
14-16.6(c)	Violation of 14-16.6(a) inflicting serious bodily injury	Class F felony
14-16.7(a)	Threatening to inflict serious bodily injury or kill executive, legislative, or court officer	Class I felony
14-16.7(b)	Depositing in mail threat to inflict serious bodily injury or kill executive, legislative, or court officer	Class I felony
Article 6: Homicide		
14-17(a)	First-degree murder	Class A felony[23]
14-17(b)	Second-degree murder[24]	Class B1 felony, except as provided below
	Based on recklessness as described in 14-17(b)(1)	Class B2 felony
	Proximately caused by unlawful distribution of opium, opiates, opioids, cocaine, methamphetamine, or other specified substance as described in 14-17(b)(2)[25]	Class B2 felony
14-18	Voluntary manslaughter	Class D felony
14-18	Involuntary manslaughter	Class F felony[26]

23. A Class A felony is punishable by death or life imprisonment for a defendant who was 18 years old or older when he or she committed first-degree murder. The death penalty is not authorized for a defendant who was under 18 years old when he or she committed first-degree murder. Roper v. Simmons, 543 U.S. 551 (2005). Instead, the punishment is either life imprisonment without parole or life imprisonment with the possibility of parole after 25 years, as determined by the court pursuant to the procedures set forth in G.S. 15A-1340.19A through -1340.19D.

24. Second-degree murder is a Class B1 felony, except it is a Class B2 felony if it was based on recklessness (*see* G.S. 14-17(b)(1)) or proximately caused by the unlawful distribution of opium, cocaine, methamphetamine, or other specified substance (*see* G.S. 14-17(b)(2)). For an offense committed before December 1, 2012, second-degree murder is punished as a Class B2 felony under G.S. 14-17 as it then existed.

25. S.L. 2017-115, effective for offenses committed on or after December 1, 2017, added deaths caused by opiates, opioids, and the depressants described in G.S. 90-92(a)(1) to this type of second-degree murder.

26. A conviction of this offense when based on impaired driving results in a permanent driver's license revocation under G.S. 20-17(a)(1), and the defendant must surrender his or her license to the court as required by G.S. 20-24(a).

Statute	Description of Offense	Punishment
Article 6A: Unborn Victims		
14-23.2(a)(1), (a)(2)	Malicious act or committing felony in 14-17 that causes death of unborn child	Class A felony
14-23.2(a)(3)	Inherently dangerous or reckless act causing death of unborn child	Punished same as second-degree murder under 14-17
14-23.3	Voluntary manslaughter of unborn child	Class D felony
14.23.4	Involuntary manslaughter of unborn child	Class F felony
14-23.5	Assault inflicting serious bodily injury on unborn child	Class F felony
Article 7A: Rape and Other Sex Offenses		
14-27.21	First-degree forcible rape[27]	Class B1 felony[28]
14-27.22	Second-degree forcible rape[29]	Class C felony[30]
14-27.23	Statutory rape of child by adult[31]	Class B1 felony; minimum sentence of at least 300 months[32]
14-27.24	First-degree statutory rape[33]	Class B1 felony[34]

27. This offense was enacted by S.L. 2015-181, effective for offenses committed on or after December 1, 2015. For offenses committed before December 1, 2015, first-degree rape committed with force is covered by G.S. 14-27.2(a)(2), repealed by this session law but with a saving clause to permit charges and prosecutions to continue to be brought.

28. This offense requires sex offender registration. G.S. 15A-1340.16B provides for life imprisonment without parole for a Class B1 felony if it was committed against a person 13 or younger, the defendant has at least one prior conviction for a Class B1 felony, and there are no mitigating factors. An indictment alleging these factors is required. If one or more of these conditions is not met, the court must sentence the defendant according to the regular structured sentencing rules.

29. This offense was enacted by S.L. 2015-181 and is effective for offenses committed on or after December 1, 2015. For offenses committed before December 1, 2015, second-degree rape with the same elements as this new statute is prohibited by G.S. 14-27.3, repealed by this session law but with a saving clause to permit charges and prosecutions to continue to be brought.

30. This offense requires sex offender registration.

31. This offense was enacted by S.L. 2015-181 and is effective for offenses committed on or after December 1, 2015. For offenses committed before December 1, 2015, statutory rape with the same elements as this new statute is prohibited by G.S. 14-27.2A, repealed by this session law but with a saving clause to permit charges and prosecutions to continue to be brought.

32. This offense requires sex offender registration. A person convicted under G.S. 14-27.23 must be sentenced to an active term of imprisonment of at least 300 months. The statutory provision purporting to allow a sentence of life without parole based on the judge's finding of egregious aggravation is an unconstitutional infringement on a defendant's Sixth Amendment right to a jury trial that may not be remedied by submitting the issue to a jury via special verdict. State v. Singletary, 247 N.C. App. 368 (2016). When released from prison, the defendant must submit to satellite-based monitoring (SBM) for life if the court determines that SBM is a reasonable search as applied to the defendant in light of *Grady v. North Carolina*, ___ U.S. ___, 135 S. Ct. 1368 (2015).

G.S. 15A-1340.16B provides for life imprisonment without parole for a Class B1 felony if it was committed against a person 13 or younger, the defendant has at least one prior conviction for a Class B1 felony, and there are no mitigating factors. An indictment alleging these factors is required. If one or more of these conditions is not met, the court must sentence the defendant according to the regular structured sentencing rules.

33. This offense was enacted by S.L. 2015-181 and is effective for offenses committed on or after December 1, 2015. For offenses committed before December 1, 2015, the elements of this offense were covered by G.S. 14-27.2(a)(1), repealed by this session law but with a saving clause to permit charges and prosecutions to continue to be brought.

34. This offense requires sex offender registration. When the General Assembly recodified sex crimes in 2015, this offense was left off the list of reportable crimes. That omission was corrected in 2017 by S.L. 2017-102, signed into law July 12, 2017,

Statute	Description of Offense	Punishment
14-27.25	Statutory rape of person 15 or younger:[35]	
	When defendant is at least 12 years old and 6 years older than person	Class B1 felony[36]
	When defendant is at least 12 years old and more than 4 but less than 6 years older than person	Class C felony[37]
14-27.26	First-degree forcible sexual offense[38]	Class B1 felony[39]
14-27.27	Second-degree forcible sexual offense[40]	Class C felony[41]
14-27.28	Statutory sexual offense with child by adult[42]	Class B1 felony; minimum sentence of at least 300 months[43]
14-27.29	First-degree statutory sexual offense[44]	Class B1 felony[45]

but retroactively effective to December 1, 2015. For offenses committed between December 1, 2015, and July 12, 2017, there may be some argument that the longer maximum sentence and post-release supervision period associated with a reportable felony cannot be added retroactively without running afoul of the Ex Post Facto Clause.

G.S. 15A-1340.16B provides for life imprisonment without parole for a Class B1 felony if it was committed against a person 13 or younger, the defendant has at least one prior conviction for a Class B1 felony, and there are no mitigating factors. An indictment alleging these factors is required. If one or more of these conditions is not met, the court must sentence the defendant according to the regular structured sentencing rules.

35. This offense was enacted by S.L. 2015-181 and is effective for offenses committed on or after December 1, 2015. For offenses committed before December 1, 2015, this offense is prohibited by G.S. 14-27.7A, repealed by this session law but with a saving clause to permit charges and prosecutions to continue to be brought.

36. This offense requires sex offender registration. G.S. 15A-1340.16B provides for life imprisonment without parole for a Class B1 felony if it was committed against a person 13 or younger, the defendant has at least one prior conviction for a Class B1 felony, and there are no mitigating factors. An indictment alleging these factors is required. If one or more of these conditions is not met, the court must sentence the defendant according to the regular structured sentencing rules.

37. This offense is not subject to sex offender registration.

38. This offense was enacted by S.L. 2015-181 and is effective for offenses committed on or after December 1, 2015. For offenses committed before December 1, 2015, first-degree sexual offense committed with force is covered by G.S. 14-27.4(a)(2), repealed by this session law but with a saving clause to permit charges and prosecutions to continue to be brought.

39. This offense requires sex offender registration. G.S. 15A-1340.16B provides for life imprisonment without parole for a Class B1 felony if it was committed against a person 13 or younger, the defendant has at least one prior conviction for a Class B1 felony, and there are no mitigating factors. An indictment alleging these factors is required. If one or more of these conditions is not met, the court must sentence the defendant according to the regular structured sentencing rules.

40. This offense was enacted by S.L. 2015-181 and is effective for offenses committed on or after December 1, 2015. For offenses committed before December 1, 2015, second-degree sexual offense committed with force is covered by G.S. 14-27.5, repealed by this session law but with a saving clause to permit charges and prosecutions to continue to be brought.

41. This offense requires sex offender registration.

42. This offense was enacted by S.L. 2015-181 and is effective for offenses committed on or after December 1, 2015. For offenses committed before December 1, 2015, statutory sexual offense with the same elements as this new statute is prohibited by G.S. 14-27.4A, repealed by this session law but with a saving clause to permit charges and prosecutions to continue to be brought.

43. *See supra* note 32.

44. This offense was enacted by S.L. 2015-181 and is effective for offenses committed on or after December 1, 2015. For offenses committed before December 1, 2015, the elements of this offense were covered by G.S. 14-27.4(a)(1), repealed by this session law but with a saving clause to permit charges and prosecutions to continue to be brought.

45. This offense requires sex offender registration. G.S. 15A-1340.16B provides for life imprisonment without parole for a Class B1 felony if it was committed against a person 13 or younger, the defendant has at least one prior conviction for a Class B1 felony, and there are no mitigating factors. An indictment alleging these factors is required. If one or more of these conditions is not met, the court must sentence the defendant according to the regular structured sentencing rules.

Statute	Description of Offense	Punishment
14-27.30	Statutory sexual offense of person 15 or younger:[46]	
	When defendant is at least 12 years old and 6 years older than person	Class B1 felony[47]
	When defendant is at least 12 years old and more than 4 but less than 6 years older than person	Class C felony[48]
14-27.31	Sexual activity by substitute parent or custodian[49]	Class E felony[50]
14-27.32	Sexual activity with student:[51]	
	By teacher, school administrator, student teacher, school safety officer, or coach	Class G felony[52]
	By other school personnel or volunteer if 4 or more years older than student	Class G felony[53]
	By other school personnel or volunteer if less than 4 years older than student	Class I felony[54]
14-27.33	Sexual battery[55]	Class A1 misdemeanor[56]

46. This offense was enacted by S.L. 2015-181 and is effective for offenses committed on or after December 1, 2015. For offenses committed before December 1, 2015, this offense is prohibited by G.S. 14-27.7A, repealed by this session law but with a saving clause to permit charges and prosecutions to continue to be brought.

47. This offense requires sex offender registration. G.S. 15A-1340.16B provides for life imprisonment without parole for a Class B1 felony if it was committed against a person 13 or younger, the defendant has at least one prior conviction for a Class B1 felony, and there are no mitigating factors. An indictment alleging these factors is required. If one or more of these conditions is not met, the court must sentence the defendant according to the regular structured sentencing rules.

48. This offense is not subject to sex offender registration.

49. This offense was enacted by S.L. 2015-181 and is effective for offenses committed on or after December 1, 2015. For offenses committed before December 1, 2015, this offense is prohibited by G.S. 14-27.7(a), repealed by this session law but with a saving clause to permit charges and prosecutions to continue to be brought. The only difference between new G.S. 14-27.31 and repealed G.S. 14-27.7(a) is G.S. 14-27.31 splits sexual activity by a substitute parent and by a custodian into subsections (a) and (b), respectively.

50. This offense requires sex offender registration.

51. This offense was enacted by S.L. 2015-181 and is effective for offenses committed on or after December 1, 2015. For offenses committed before December 1, 2015, this offense is prohibited by G.S. 14-27.7(b), repealed by this session law but with a saving clause to permit charges and prosecutions to continue to be brought. The only difference between new G.S. 14-27.32 and repealed G.S. 14-27.7(b) is G.S. 14-27.32 splits the Class G felonies into subsection (a) and the Class I felony into subsection (b).

52. This offense requires sex offender registration.

53. This offense requires sex offender registration.

54. This offense requires sex offender registration. Amended G.S. 14-27.7(b) (school personnel, other than teacher, school administrator, student teacher, school safety officer, or coach, who is less than 4 years older than student victim, commits vaginal intercourse or a sexual act with student), recodified later as G.S. 14-27.32(b) by S.L. 2015-181, increases the punishment from a Class A1 misdemeanor to a Class I felony. This provision is effective for offenses committed on or after December 1, 2015. Although this punishment change was not carried forward in the statutory language in new G.S. 14-27.32(b), as recodified by S.L. 2015-181, it still became law based on the provisions of G.S. 120-20.1(b1).

55. S.L. 2015-181 recodified this offense without any changes from G.S. 14-27.5A to G.S. 14-27.33, effective for offenses committed on or after December 1, 2015. A saving clause permits charges and prosecutions to continue to be brought under G.S. 14-27.5A for offenses committed before December 1, 2015.

56. This offense requires sex offender registration.

Statute	Description of Offense	Punishment
Article 8: Assaults		
14-28	Malicious castration	Class C felony
14-29	Castration or maiming	Class E felony
14-30	Malicious maiming of tongue or eye	Class C felony
14-30.1	Malicious acid throwing	Class E felony
14-31	Assault and battery in secret manner with deadly weapon with intent to kill	Class E felony[57]
14-32(a)	Assault with deadly weapon with intent to kill, inflicting serious injury	Class C felony[58]
14-32(b)	Assault with deadly weapon, inflicting serious injury	Class E felony[59]
14-32(c)	Assault with deadly weapon with intent to kill	Class E felony[60]
14-32.1(e)(1)	Assault on handicapped person with deadly weapon or other means of force likely to inflict serious injury or damage	Class F felony[61]
14-32.1(e)(2)	Assault on handicapped person inflicting serious injury or damage	Class F felony
14-32.1(e)(3)	Assault on handicapped person with intent to kill	Class F felony
14-32.1(f)	Simple assault on handicapped person	Class A1 misdemeanor
14-32.2(b)(1), (a)	Patient abuse: intentional conduct resulting in death	Class C felony
14-32.2(b)(2), (a)	Patient abuse: culpably negligent conduct resulting in death	Class E felony
14-32.2(b)(3), (a)	Patient abuse: conduct resulting in serious bodily injury	Class F felony
14-32.2(b)(4), (a)	Patient abuse: pattern of conduct resulting in bodily injury	Class H felony
14-32.3(a)	Abuse by caretaker of disabled or elder adult residing in domestic setting:	
	Resulting in serious injury	Class F felony
	Resulting in injury	Class H felony

57. If the assault was committed with a motor vehicle, a conviction results in a mandatory one-year DMV driver's license revocation under G.S. 20-17(a)(11). A defendant must surrender his or her driver's license to the court as required by G.S. 20-24(a).
58. *See supra* note 57.
59. *See supra* note 57.
60. *See supra* note 57.
61. *See supra* note 57.

Statute	Description of Offense	Punishment
14-32.3(b)	Neglect by caretaker of disabled or elder adult residing in domestic setting:	
	Resulting in serious injury	Class G felony
	Resulting in injury	Class I felony
14-32.4(a)	Assault inflicting serious bodily injury	Class F felony
14.32.4(b)	Assault by strangulation	Class H felony
14-33(a)	Simple assault, simple assault and battery, or simple affray	Class 2 misdemeanor
14-33(b)(9)	Assault and battery on sports official	Class 1 misdemeanor
14-33(c)(1)	Assault:	
	Inflicting serious injury	Class A1 misdemeanor
	With deadly weapon	Class A1 misdemeanor[62]
14-33(c)(2)	Assault on female	Class A1 misdemeanor
14-33(c)(3)	Assault on child under 12	Class A1 misdemeanor
14-33(c)(4)	Assault on government official	Class A1 misdemeanor
14-33(c)(6)	Assault on school employee or volunteer	Class A1 misdemeanor
14-33(c)(7)	Assault on public transit operator	Class A1 misdemeanor
14-33(c)(8)	Assault on company or campus police officer	Class A1 misdemeanor
14-33(d)	Assault in presence of minor on person with whom defendant has personal relationship:[63]	
	Inflicting serious injury	Class A1 misdemeanor
	With deadly weapon	Class A1 misdemeanor
14-33.2	Habitual misdemeanor assault	Class H felony
14-34	Assault by pointing gun	Class A1 misdemeanor
14-34.1(a)	Discharging or attempting to discharge firearm into occupied property	Class E felony
14-34.1(b)	Discharging or attempting to discharge firearm into occupied dwelling or occupied conveyance in operation	Class D felony
14-34.1(c)	Violation of 14-34.1(a) or (b) resulting in serious bodily injury	Class C felony

62. If the assault was committed with a motor vehicle, a conviction results in a mandatory one-year DMV driver's license revocation under G.S. 20-17(a)(11). A defendant must surrender his or her driver's license to the court as required by G.S. 20-24(a).

63. If the court sentences a person to a community punishment, the court must place the person on supervised probation in addition to any other punishment; for a second or subsequent violation, the court must sentence the person to an active punishment of no less than 30 days in addition to any other punishment. *See* G.S. 14-33(d).

Statute	Description of Offense	Punishment
14-34.2	Assault with deadly weapon on government official or on company or campus police officer	Class F felony[64]
14-34.4(a)	Tampering with food, drugs, or cosmetics with intent to cause serious injury or death	Class C felony
14-34.4(b)	Threatening to tamper with food, drugs, or cosmetics with intent to extort	Class C felony
14-34.5	Assault with firearm on law enforcement, probation, or parole officer, detention facility employee, or member of the North Carolina National Guard	Class E felony
14-34.6(a)	Assault or affray on a firefighter, an emergency medical technician, medical responder, or hospital personnel causing physical injury [65]	Class I felony
14-34.6(b)	Assault or affray on a firefighter, an emergency medical technician, medical responder, or hospital personnel inflicting serious bodily injury or with deadly weapon other than firearm[66]	Class H felony
14-34.6(c)	Assault causing physical injury on firefighter, emergency personnel, or hospital personnel when using firearm[67]	Class F felony
14-34.7(a)	Assault inflicting serious injury or serious bodily injury on law enforcement, probation, or parole officer	Class F felony
14-34.7(a1)	Assault inflicting serious injury or serious bodily injury on North Carolina National Guard member	Class F felony
14-34.7(b)	Assault inflicting serious injury or serious bodily injury on detention facility employee	Class F felony
14-34.7(c)(1)	Assault inflicting physical injury on law enforcement, probation, or parole officer	Class I felony
14-34.7(c)(2)	Assault inflicting physical injury on detention facility employee	Class I felony
14-34.7(c)(3)	Assault inflicting physical injury on North Carolina National Guard member	Class I felony
14-34.8, -3.1(a)	Pointing laser device at law enforcement officer or at head or face of other person	Infraction

64. If the assault was committed with a motor vehicle, a conviction results in a mandatory one-year DMV driver's license revocation under G.S. 20-17(a)(11). A defendant must surrender his or her driver's license to the court as required by G.S. 20-24(a).

65. S.L. 2017-57, effective for offenses committed on or after December 1, 2017, added hospital security personnel to this offense.

66. *See supra* note 65.

67. *See supra* note 65.

Statute	Description of Offense	Punishment
14-34.9	Discharging firearm from enclosure as part of pattern of criminal street gang activity	Class E felony
14-34.10	Discharging firearm within enclosure to incite fear	Class F felony

Article 9: Hazing

14-35	Hazing	Class 2 misdemeanor

Article 10: Kidnapping and Abduction

14-39	Kidnapping:	
	First-degree	Class C felony[68]
	Second-degree	Class E felony[69]
Common law	False imprisonment	Class 1 misdemeanor under 14-3(a)
14-41	Abduction of minor	Class F felony[70]
14-43.3	Felonious restraint	Class F felony[71]

Article 10A: Human Trafficking[72]

14-43.11	Human trafficking:[73]	
	Of adult	Class C felony[74]
	Of minor	Class B2 felony[75]
14-43.12(a), (b)	Involuntary servitude:	
	Of adult	Class F felony
	Of minor	Class C felony
14-43.12(e)	Failure of party to labor contract to report involuntary servitude	Class 1 misdemeanor

68. This offense requires sex offender registration when committed against a minor by a defendant who is not the minor's parent.

69. *See supra* note 68.

70. *See supra* note 68.

71. *See supra* note 68.

72. Violations of this Article are subject to the special restitution and property forfeiture provisions in G.S. 14-43.20.

73. G.S. 14-43.20 provides for mandatory restitution as set out in the statute and subjects the defendant to the property forfeiture provisions in G.S. 14-2.3.

74. This offense was increased from a Class F to a Class C felony by S.L. 2017-151, effective for offenses committed on or after December 1, 2017. This offense requires sex offender registration if committed against any person with the intent that they be held in sexual servitude. G.S. 14-208.6(5).

75. This offense was increased from a Class C to a Class B2 felony by S.L. 2017-151, effective for offenses committed on or after December 1, 2017. This offense requires sex offender registration.

Statute	Description of Offense	Punishment
14-43.13	Sexual servitude:	
	Of adult	Class D felony[76]
	Of minor	Class C felony[77]
14-43.14	Unlawful sale, surrender, or purchase of a minor:[78]	
	First offense	Class F felony with minimum $5,000 fine
	Subsequent offense	Class F felony with minimum $10,000 fine

Article 11: Abortion and Kindred Offenses

14-44	Using drugs or instruments with intent to cause abortion	Class H felony
14-45	Using drugs or instruments with intent to produce miscarriage or injure pregnant woman	Class I felony
14-46	Concealing birth of child:	
	Concealing	Class I felony
	Aiding or abetting another in concealing	Class 1 misdemeanor
14-46.1	Selling remains of unborn child resulting from abortion or miscarriage	Class I felony

Article 12: Libel and Slander

14-47	Communicating libelous matter to newspaper	Class 2 misdemeanor

Article 13: Malicious Injury or Damage by Use of Explosive or Incendiary Device or Material

14-49(a)	Malicious use of explosive or incendiary device to injure another	Class D felony
14-49(b)	Malicious use of explosive to damage property	Class G felony[79]
14-49(b1)	Malicious use of explosive to damage building of worship	Class E felony[80]
14-49(b2)	Malicious use of explosive to damage government building	Class E felony

76. This offense requires sex offender registration.
77. This offense requires sex offender registration.
78. This offense requires sex offender registration only if the court rules that the defendant is a danger to the community and that registration would further the purposes of Article 27A of Chapter 14.
79. A conviction of this offense results in a mandatory one-year DMV driver's license revocation under G.S. 20-17(a)(15), and for a driver under 18, G.S. 20-13.2(c2), (d). A defendant must surrender his or her driver's license to the court as required by G.S. 20-24(a).
80. *See supra* note 79.

Statute	Description of Offense	Punishment
14-49.1	Malicious use of explosive or incendiary device to damage occupied property	Class D felony

Article 13A: North Carolina Gang Suppression Act[81]

Statute	Description of Offense	Punishment
14-50.17	Solicitation of person 16 or older to participate in criminal gang activity	Class H felony
14-50.18	Solicitation of person under 16 to participate in criminal gang activity	Class F felony
14-50.19(a)	Threatening to injure person or damage property with intent to deter person from assisting another to withdraw from criminal gang	Class G felony[82]
14-50.19(a1)	Injuring a person with the intent to deter a person from assisting another to withdraw from membership in a criminal gang	Class F felony[83]
14-50.20(a)	Threatening to injure person or damage property in retaliation against person for having withdrawn from criminal gang	Class G felony[84]

---

81. **Conditional discharge.** G.S. 14-50.29 provides for a conditional discharge for first offenders under the age of 18 when the offense was committed and the offense was a Class H felony under the article or an enhanced offense under G.S. 14-50.22.

Enhancement. Effective for offenses committed on or after December 1, 2017, G.S. 15A-1340.16E provides that if an offense was committed as part of criminal gang activity, the person may be charged and sentenced one felony class higher than the principal felony for which the person was convicted. If the person is a criminal gang leader or organizer, the class is two classes higher than the principal felony. The sentence can be no higher than a Class C felony, and any sentence must run consecutively with and must commence at the expiration of any sentence then being served. The enhancement does not apply to a gang offense in Article 13A of G.S. Chapter 14. The indictment or information for the felony must allege in that pleading the facts that qualify the offense for enhancement; one pleading is sufficient for all felonies tried at a single trial. The State must prove the facts beyond a reasonable doubt; the procedures for determining aggravating factors in G.S. 15A-1340.16(a1), (a2), and (a3) apply.

Forfeiture. G.S. 14-2.3 provides for the forfeiture of any money or other property acquired in the case of any violation of Article 13A, while G.S. 14-50.23 provides for the forfeiture of the proceeds of criminal gang activity or a pattern of criminal gang activity and includes an exception for innocent activities. G.S. 14-50.25 provides that when a defendant is found guilty of an offense other than a violation of G.S. 14-50.16 through -50.20, the judge must determine whether the offense involved criminal gang activity and, if the judge so finds, indicate that fact on the judgment form; there is no additional punishment prescribed in those circumstances. G.S. 14-50.26 provides that a conviction of an offense defined as criminal gang activity precludes the defendant from contesting any factual matters determined in the criminal proceeding in any subsequent civil action or proceeding based on the same conduct.

Under Article 13B (North Carolina Criminal Gang Nuisance Abatement Act), effective October 1, 2012, any real property used by a criminal gang for conducting criminal gang activity constitutes a public nuisance and is subject to abatement as provided in Article 1 (abatement of nuisances) of Chapter 19. There is an exception for owners or possessors who do not have actual knowledge of the activity and for coerced owners. *See* G.S. 14-50.42. G.S. 14-50.43 provides that a gang that regularly engages in criminal gang activities constitutes a public nuisance, and any person who regularly associates with others to engage in such activity may be made a defendant in a nuisance abatement suit. Upon finding a public nuisance, the court may enter an order enjoining the defendant from engaging in criminal gang activities and may impose other reasonable requirements to prevent future activities. Any order entered expires one year after entry, and the order may be modified or vacated upon motion of any party before that time.

82. S.L. 2017-194, effective for offenses committed on or after December 1, 2017, increased the punishment for this offense from a Class H felony to a Class G felony.

83. This offense was enacted by S.L. 2017-194, effective for offenses committed on or after December 1, 2017.

84. S.L. 2017-194, effective for offenses committed on or after December 1, 2017, increased the punishment for this offense from a Class H felony to a Class G felony.

Statute	Description of Offense	Punishment
14-50.20(a1)	Injuring a person as punishment or retaliation against a person for having withdrawn from a criminal gang	Class F felony[85]
14-50.22	Misdemeanor committed by person 15 or older on behalf of criminal gang	Punishable one class higher than misdemeanor committed[86]

Article 14: Burglary and Other Housebreakings

14-51, -52	Burglary:	
	First-degree	Class D felony
	Second-degree	Class G felony
14-53	Breaking out of dwelling house	Class D felony
14-54(a)	Breaking or entering building with intent to commit felony or larceny	Class H felony
14-54(a1)	Breaking or entering building with intent to terrorize or injure occupant	Class H felony
14-54(b)	Misdemeanor breaking or entering building	Class 1 misdemeanor
14-54.1	Breaking or entering place of worship	Class G felony
14-55	Preparation to commit breaking or entering	Class I felony
14-56	Breaking or entering car, boat, airplane, etc., with intent to commit felony or larceny	Class I felony
14-56.1	Breaking into coin/currency-operated machine:	
	First offense	Class 1 misdemeanor
	Subsequent offense	Class I felony
14-56.2	Damaging coin/currency-operated machine	Class 1 misdemeanor
14-56.3	Breaking into paper currency machine:	
	First offense	Class 1 misdemeanor
	Subsequent offense	Class I felony
14-56.4(b), (d)	Unlawfully possessing motor vehicle master key or other lock-picking device:	
	First offense	Class 1 misdemeanor
	Subsequent offense under 14-56.4	Class I felony

85. This offense was enacted by S.L. 2017-194, effective for offenses committed on or after December 1, 2017.
86. A Class A1 misdemeanor is enhanced to a Class I felony.

Statute	Description of Offense	Punishment
14-56.4(c), (d)	Unlawfully buying, selling, or transferring motor vehicle master key or other lock-picking device:	
	First offense	Class 1 misdemeanor
	Subsequent offense under 14-56.4	Class I felony
14-57	Burglary with explosive	Class D felony

Article 15: Arson and Other Burnings

Statute	Description of Offense	Punishment
14-58	Arson:	
	First-degree	Class D felony
	Second-degree	Class G felony
14-59	Burning public building	Class F felony
14-60	Burning educational building	Class F felony
14-61	Burning bridges, certain buildings	Class F felony
14-62	Burning uninhabited dwellings, certain other buildings	Class F felony
14-62.1	Burning building under construction	Class H felony
14-62.2	Burning church, chapel, or meetinghouse	Class E felony
14-63	Burning boat or barge	Class H felony
14-64	Burning ginhouse or tobacco house	Class H felony
14-65	Burning dwelling house owned or occupied by defendant	Class H felony
14-66	Burning personal property	Class H felony
14-67.1	Burning building not otherwise covered by statute	Class H felony
14-67.2(a)	Burning during the commission of a felony that results in damage of $10,000 or more	Class D felony[87]
14-67.2(b)	Aiding or abetting, during the commission of a felony, burning that results in damage of $10,000 or more	Class D felony[88]
14-69.1(a)	Making false report of explosive in or near building or structure	Class H felony[89]

87. This offense was enacted by S.L. 2018-31, effective for offenses committed on or after December 1, 2018.
88. This offense was enacted by S.L. 2018-31, effective for offenses committed on or after December 1, 2018.
89. The court may order a convicted defendant to pay restitution for disruption of normal activities on the premises.

Statute	Description of Offense	Punishment
14-69.1(c)	Making false report of explosive in or near public building:[90]	
	First offense	Class H felony
	Subsequent conviction within five years of first conviction	Class G felony
14-69.2(a)	Perpetrating hoax by use of false bomb	Class H felony[91]
14-69.2(c)	Perpetrating hoax by use of false bomb in public building:[92]	
	First offense	Class H felony
	Subsequent conviction within five years of first conviction	Class G felony
14-69.3	Arson or other felony under Ch. 14, Art. 15, resulting in serious bodily injury to firefighter, law enforcement officer, fire investigator, or emergency medical technician[93]	Class E felony

Article 16: Larceny[94]

Statute	Description of Offense	Punishment
14-70, -72(a)	Larceny:	
	Of goods valued up to $1,000	Class 1 misdemeanor
	Of goods valued over $1,000	Class H felony
14-70, -72(a), (b)(1)	Larceny from person	Class H felony
14-70, -72(a), (b)(2)	Larceny pursuant to burglary or breaking or entering in violation of 14-51, -53, -54, -54.1, or -57	Class H felony
14-70, -72(a), (b)(3)	Larceny of explosive or incendiary device or substance	Class H felony
14-70, -72(a), (b)(4)	Larceny of firearm	Class H felony
14-70, -72(a), (b)(5)	Larceny of record or paper in custody of State Archives	Class H felony

90. *See supra* note 89. A conviction of this offense results in a mandatory DMV driver's license revocation for one year under G.S. 20-17(a)(15), and for a driver under 18, G.S. 20-13.2(c2), (d). A defendant must surrender his or her driver's license to the court as required by G.S. 20-24(a).

91. *See supra* note 89.

92. *See supra* note 89. A conviction of this offense results in a mandatory DMV driver's license revocation for one year under G.S. 20-17(a)(15), and for a driver under 18, G.S. 20-13.2(c2), (d). A defendant must surrender his or her driver's license to the court as required by G.S. 20-24(a).

93. S.L. 2018-31, effective for offenses committed on or after December 1, 2018, added law enforcement officers and fire investagors to this offense.

94. Conveyances used to conceal, convey, or transport property in violation of G.S. 14-71 (receiving stolen goods) or G.S. 14-71.1 (possession of stolen goods) used in violation of G.S. 14-72.7 (chop shop activity) or used in the commission of any larceny when the value of the property taken is more than $2,000 are subject to forfeiture as provided in G.S. 14-86.1.

Statute	Description of Offense	Punishment
14-70, -72(a), (b)(6)	Larceny committed after four previous larceny convictions	Class H felony
14-71(a), -72(a)	Receiving:	
	Stolen goods valued up to $1,000	Class 1 misdemeanor
	Stolen goods valued over $1,000	Class H felony
14-71(a), -72(c)	Receiving:	
	Goods stolen from a person	Class H felony
	Goods stolen pursuant to burglary or breaking or entering in violation of 14-51, -53, -54, -54.1, or -57	Class H felony
	Stolen explosive or incendiary device or substance	Class H felony
	Stolen firearm	Class H felony
	Stolen record or paper in custody of State Archives	Class H felony
14-71(b)	Receiving or possessing property in custody of law enforcement agency that was represented to be stolen	Class H felony
14-71.1, -72(a)	Possession:	
	Of stolen goods valued up to $1,000	Class 1 misdemeanor
	Of stolen goods valued over $1,000	Class H felony
14-71.1, -72(c)	Possession:	
	Of goods stolen from a person	Class H felony
	Of goods stolen pursuant to burglary or breaking or entering in violation of 14-51, -53, -54, -54.1, or -57	Class H felony
	Of stolen explosive or incendiary device or substance	Class H felony
	Of stolen firearm	Class H felony
	Of stolen record or paper in custody of State Archives	Class H felony

Statute	Description of Offense	Punishment
14-72.1(a), (e)	Willful concealment of merchandise:	
	First offense	Class 3 misdemeanor[95]
	Second offense within three years of first conviction under 14-72.1	Class 2 misdemeanor[96]
	Third or subsequent offense within five years of two prior convictions under 14-72.1	Class 1 misdemeanor[97]
	Subsequent offense not falling into above two categories	Class 3 misdemeanor[98]
14-72.1(d), (e)	Switching price tags:	
	First offense	Class 3 misdemeanor[99]
	Second offense within three years of first conviction under 14-72.1	Class 2 misdemeanor[100]
	Third or subsequent offense within five years of two prior convictions under 14-72.1	Class 1 misdemeanor[101]
	Subsequent offense not falling into above two categories	Class 3 misdemeanor[102]
14-72.1(d1), (a)	Willful concealment of merchandise by lead/aluminum-lined device	Class H felony
14-72.2	Unauthorized use:	
	Of motor vehicle, motorboat, or other motor-propelled conveyance	Class 1 misdemeanor
	Of aircraft	Class H felony
14-72.3	Unauthorized removal of shopping cart from shopping premises	Class 3 misdemeanor
14-72.4	Unauthorized taking or sale of labeled milk crate	Class 2 misdemeanor
14-72.5	Larceny of gasoline valued at less than $1,000	Class 1 misdemeanor[103]

95. G.S. 14-72.1(e) provides that the term of imprisonment may be suspended only on condition that the defendant perform community service for at least 24 hours. If the judge finds that the defendant is unable to perform community service because of a mental or physical infirmity, the judge may impose such other sentence as he or she finds appropriate, provided the judge sets out the reasons for this finding in the judgment.

96. G.S. 14-72.1(e) provides that the term of imprisonment may be suspended only on condition that the defendant be imprisoned for at least 72 hours as a condition of special probation, perform community service for at least 72 hours, or both. If the judge finds that the defendant is unable to perform community service because of a mental or physical infirmity, the judge may impose such other sentence as he or she finds appropriate, provided that the judge sets out the reasons for this finding in the judgment.

97. G.S. 14-72.1(e) provides that the term of imprisonment may be suspended only if a condition of special probation is that the defendant serve a term of imprisonment of at least 11 days.

98. *See supra* note 95.

99. *See supra* note 95.

100. *See supra* note 96.

101. *See supra* note 97.

102. *See supra* note 95.

103. A second conviction within seven years results in a mandatory 90-day DMV driver's license revocation; a third or subsequent conviction results in a mandatory six-month revocation. *See* G.S. 20-17(a)(16), G.S. 20-19(g2); *see also*

Statute	Description of Offense	Punishment
14-72.6(a)(1)	Larceny of construction materials worth more than $300 and less than $1,000 from permitted construction site	Class I felony
14-72.6(a)(2)	Receiving or possessing construction materials worth more than $300 and less than $1,000 stolen from permitted construction site	Class I felony
14-72.7	Chop shop activity:[104]	
	Altering, destroying, dismantling, or storing a motor vehicle or part known to be illegally obtained	Class G felony
	Permitting place to be used for illegal activity under 14-72.7	Class G felony
	Purchasing, disposing of, selling, receiving, or possessing a motor vehicle or part knowing that the vehicle ID number has been altered	Class G felony
	Purchasing, disposing of, selling, receiving, or possessing a motor vehicle or part to or from person engaged in illegal activity under 14-72.7	Class G felony
14-72.8	Felony larceny of motor vehicle parts if repair costs $1,000 or more	Class I felony
14-72.11	Larceny from merchant:	
	By use of certain exit doors when property has value of more than $200	Class H felony
	By removing, destroying, or deactivating antishoplifting or inventory control device	Class H felony
	By affixing product code for purpose of fraudulently obtaining goods at less than actual price	Class H felony
	When property is infant formula and has value of more than $100	Class H felony
	By exchanging property for cash, a gift card, a merchandise card, or some other item of value, knowing or having reasonable grounds to believe the property is stolen[105]	Class H felony

G.S. 20-16(e2) (authorizing limited privilege). For both mandatory revocations, a defendant must surrender his or her driver's license to the court as required by G.S. 20-24(a).

104. G.S. 14-72.7 authorizes the following additional remedies: (1) the criminal court may assess a civil penalty, in addition to or in lieu of a fine, of up to three times the assets obtained by the defendant as a result of the violation, to be remitted to the Civil Penalty and Forfeiture Fund, (2) a person aggrieved by a violation may file a civil action for damages, and (3) any instrumentality used in a prohibited activity is subject to seizure and forfeiture under G.S. 14-86.1, and the real property used for a prohibited activity is subject to abatement and forfeiture under Chapter 19.

105. This version of the offense was added to the law by S.L. 2017-162, effective for offenses committed on or after December 1, 2017.

Statute	Description of Offense	Punishment
14-74	Larceny or embezzlement by employee:	
	Of less than $100,000	Class H felony
	Of $100,000 or more	Class C felony
14-75	Larceny of chose in action	Class H felony
14-75.1	Larceny of secret technical process	Class H felony
14-76	Larceny of public records or papers	Class 1 misdemeanor
14-77	Larceny of will	Class 1 misdemeanor
14-78	Larceny of ungathered crops	Class H felony
14-79	Larceny of ginseng	Class H felony
14-79.1	Larceny of pine straw	Class H felony
14-79.2(a), (b)	Waste kitchen grease offense:	
	Value of container or container and grease therein is $1,000 or less	Class 1 misdemeanor
	Value is $1,000 or more	Class H felony
14-81(a)	Larceny of horse, mule, swine, or cattle	Class H felony[106]
14-81(a1)	Larceny of a dog	Class I felony[107]
14-82	Temporarily taking horse, mule, or dog	Class 2 misdemeanor
14-86.2	Taking or vandalizing chemical or portable toilet or pumper truck operated by permitted management firm	Class 1 misdemeanor

Article 16A: Organized Retail Theft[108]

Statute	Description of Offense	Punishment
14-86.6(a)(1)	Organized retail theft	Class H felony[109]
14-86.6(a)(2)	Receiving or possessing retail property taken in violation of 14-86.6(a)(1)	Class H felony[110]
14-86.6(a1)(1)	Conspiring with another to commit theft of retail property with a value exceeding $20,000 aggregated over a 90-day period	Class G felony[111]

---

106. G.S. 14-81(b) provides that the minimum sentence for this offense is probation subject to the following conditions: (1) restitution for the damage or loss caused by the larceny and (2) a fine of not less than the amount of damages or loss caused by the larceny.

107. *See supra* note 106.

108. Under G.S. 14-86.6(c), effective for offenses committed on or after December 1, 2017, thefts of retail property occurring in more than one county may be aggregated into an alleged violation of G.S. 14-86.6.

109. G.S. 14-86.6(b) provides that any interest acquired or maintained in violation of G.S. 14-86.6 is subject to forfeiture as provided in G.S. 18B-504 under the alcoholic beverage control laws.

110. *See supra* note 109.

111. This offense was enacted by S.L. 2017-162, effective for offenses committed on or after December 1, 2017.

Statute	Description of Offense	Punishment
14-86.6(a1)(2)	Conspiring with two or more other persons as an organizer, supervisor, financier, leader, or manager to engage in organized retail theft	Class G felony[112]

Article 17: Robbery[113]

Statute	Description of Offense	Punishment
14-87	Armed robbery or attempted armed robbery	Class D felony
14-87.1	Common law robbery	Class G felony
14-88	Train robbery	Class D felony
14-89.1	Safecracking or attempted safecracking	Class I felony

Article 18: Embezzlement

Statute	Description of Offense	Punishment
14-90	Embezzlement by agent or fiduciary:	
	Of less than $100,000	Class H felony
	Of $100,000 or more	Class C felony
14-91	Embezzlement of state property by public officer or employee:	
	Of less than $100,000	Class F felony
	Of $100,000 or more	Class C felony
14-92	Embezzlement by public officer or trustee:	
	Of less than $100,000	Class F felony
	Of $100,000 or more	Class C felony
14-93	Embezzlement by treasurer of charitable or religious organization:	
	Of less than $100,000	Class H felony
	Of $100,000 or more	Class C felony
14-94	Embezzlement by officer of railroad company:	
	Of less than $100,000	Class H felony
	Of $100,000 or more	Class C felony
14-97	Appropriation of partnership funds by partner:	
	Of less than $100,000	Class H felony
	Of $100,000 or more	Class C felony

112. This offense was enacted by S.L. 2017-162, effective for offenses committed on or after December 1, 2017.
113. Conveyances used in the commission of armed or common law robbery are subject to forfeiture as provided in G.S. 14-86.1.

Statute	Description of Offense	Punishment
14-98	Embezzlement by surviving partner, with refusal to account for funds:	
	Of less than $100,000	Class H felony
	Of $100,000 or more	Class C felony
14-99	Embezzlement of taxes by public officer:	
	Of less than $100,000	Class F felony
	Of $100,000 or more	Class C felony

Article 19: False Pretenses and Cheats

14-100	Obtaining or attempting to obtain property by false pretenses:	
	Of less than $100,000	Class H felony
	Of $100,000 or more	Class C felony
14-100.1(a), (e)	Possession or manufacture of fraudulent identification	Class 1 misdemeanor
14-100.1(b), (e)	Obtaining form of identification by use of fraudulent information	Class 1 misdemeanor
14-101	Obtaining signature by false pretenses	Class H felony
14-104	Obtaining advance by false promise to work	Class 2 misdemeanor
14-105	Obtaining advance by false written promise to pay out of designated property	Class 2 misdemeanor
14-106	Obtaining property by worthless check	Class 3 misdemeanor
14-107	Knowingly writing worthless check over $2,000	Class I felony[114]
14-107(d)(1)	Knowingly writing worthless check of $2,000 or less	Class 3 misdemeanor[115]
14-107(d)(3)	Knowingly writing worthless check on nonexistent account	Class 1 misdemeanor[116]
14-107(d)(4)	Knowingly writing worthless check on closed account	Class 1 misdemeanor[117]
14-110	Defrauding innkeeper or restaurant owner	Class 2 misdemeanor
14-111.4	Misuse of 911 system	Class 1 misdemeanor

114. G.S. 14-107(e) provides that the judge, in imposing any sentence other than an active term of imprisonment, may require the defendant to pay as part of the costs a witness fee for each prosecuting witness and to make restitution to the victim for (1) the amount of the check, (2) any service charges imposed on the payee by a bank for processing the dishonored check, and (3) any processing fees imposed by the payee in compliance with G.S. 25-3-506.

115. A defendant who has previously been convicted three times of violating G.S. 14-107 shall be punished for this offense as for a Class 1 misdemeanor; if placed on probation, the defendant shall be ordered to refrain from maintaining a checking account or making or uttering a check for three years. *See* G.S. 14-107(d)(1). In imposing any sentence other than an active term of imprisonment, the judge may require the defendant to pay costs and make restitution as described in note 114.

116. *See supra* note 114.

117. *See supra* note 114.

Statute	Description of Offense	Punishment
14-112	Obtaining merchandise on approval with intent to defraud	Class 2 misdemeanor
14-112.2(b), (d)	Exploitation of older or disabled adult through position of trust or business relationship if property is worth:	
	$100,000 or more	Class F felony
	$20,000 or more and less than $100,000	Class G felony
	Less than $20,000	Class H felony
14-112.2(c), (e)	Exploitation of older or disabled adult lacking capacity if property is worth:	
	$100,000 or more	Class G felony
	$20,000 or more and less than $100,000	Class H felony
	Less than $20,000	Class I felony
14-113	Obtaining money by false representation of physical disability	Class 2 misdemeanor

Article 19A: Obtaining Property or Services by False or Fraudulent Use of Credit Device or Other Means

Statute	Description of Offense	Punishment
14-113.1, -113.6	Obtaining or attempting to obtain goods through false telephone number, credit number, or credit device	Class 2 misdemeanor
14-113.4, -113.6	Avoiding or attempting to avoid lawful charges for telecommunications services	Class 2 misdemeanor
14-113.5, -113.6	Unlawful use of telecommunications services	Class 2 misdemeanor[118]

Article 19B: Financial Transaction Card Crime Act

Statute	Description of Offense	Punishment
14-113.9, -113.17(b)	Theft of financial transaction card	Class I felony
14-113.11, 113.17(b)	Forgery of financial transaction card	Class I felony
14-113.13(a), (b), -113.17	Financial transaction card fraud:	
	When value obtained in six-month period is $500 or less	Class 2 misdemeanor
	When value obtained in six-month period exceeds $500	Class I felony
14-113.13(c), -113.17(a)	False statement on application for financial transaction card	Class 2 misdemeanor
14-113.13(c1), -113.17(a)	False record of sale submitted by person authorized to accept financial transaction card	Class 2 misdemeanor

118. G.S. 14-113.6(a) provides that a violation of G.S. 14-113.5 is a Class G felony if it involves five or more unlawful telecommunications devices, and G.S. 14-113.6(b) provides that a court may order restitution for a violation of G.S. 14-113.5.

Statute	Description of Offense	Punishment
14-113.13(d), -113.17(a)	False report of loss of financial transaction card	Class 2 misdemeanor
14-113.14, -113.17(b)	Criminal possession of financial transaction card forgery device	Class I felony
14-113.15, -113.17	Criminal receipt of goods or services obtained by financial transaction card fraud:	
	When value obtained in six-month period is $500 or less	Class 2 misdemeanor
	When value obtained in six-month period exceeds $500	Class I felony
14-113.15A, -113.17(b)	Criminal factoring of financial transaction card records	Class I felony

Article 19C: Identity Theft

Statute	Description of Offense	Punishment
14-113.20, -113.22(a)	Financial identity theft	Class G felony [119]
14-113.20A, -113.22(a1)	Trafficking in stolen identities	Class E felony [120]
14-113.24	Printing more than five digits of account number on credit charge or debit card receipt	Infraction [121]

Article 19D: Telephone Records Privacy Protection Act

Statute	Description of Offense	Punishment
14-113.31(a), -113.33	Obtaining or attempting to obtain customer's telephone record without consent	Class H felony [122]
14-113.31(b), -113.33	Purchasing or receiving, or soliciting another to purchase or receive, customer's telephone record without authorization	Class H felony [123]
14-113.31(c), -113.33	Selling or offering to sell telephone record that was obtained without customer's consent	Class H felony [124]

---

119. Under G.S. 14-113.22(a), financial identity theft is punishable as a Class F felony if (1) the victim (that is, the person whose personal identifying information is fraudulently used) is arrested, detained, or convicted as a result of the offense or (2) the defendant is in possession of the identifying information of three or more people. The court also may order restitution for financial loss caused by the violation to any person as provided in G.S. 14-113.22(a2), and the victim may bring a civil suit for damages, injunctive relief, and attorneys' fees as provided in G.S. 14-113.22(b) and G.S. 1-539.2C.

120. The court may order restitution for financial loss caused by the violation to any person as provided in G.S. 14-113.22(a2), and the victim may bring a civil suit for damages, injunctive relief, and attorneys' fees as provided in G.S. 14-113.22(b) and G.S. 1-539.2C.

121. A violation is subject to a penalty up to $500 per violation, not to exceed $500 per calendar month and $2,000 per calendar year.

122. A violation of G.S. 14-113.31 is a violation of G.S. 75-1.1, allowing a customer to bring a civil action for damages or $1,000, whichever is greater. *See* G.S. 14-113.33(b).

123. *See supra* note 122.

124. *See supra* note 122.

Statute	Description of Offense	Punishment
Article 20: Frauds		
14-114	Fraudulent disposal or purchase of collateral	Class 2 misdemeanor
14-115	Secreting property to hinder enforcement of security interest	Class 2 misdemeanor
14-117	Fraudulent and deceptive advertising	Class 2 misdemeanor
14-118	Blackmail	Class 1 misdemeanor
14-118.1	Simulation of court process in connection with collection of claim, demand, or account	Class I felony
14-118.2	Assisting in obtaining academic credit by fraudulent means	Class 2 misdemeanor
14-118.4	Extortion	Class F felony
14-118.5(a)	Unauthorized interception of cable television service	Class 3 misdemeanor[125]
14-118.5(b)	Unauthorized sale of decoder for cable television signal	Class 3 misdemeanor[126]
14-118.6(a)	Knowingly filing false lien or encumbrance against public officer's or public employee's property	Class I felony
14-118.7	Possession, transfer, or use of automated sales suppression device	Class H felony[127]
Article 20A: Residential Mortgage Fraud Act		
14-118.12, -118.15	Residential mortgage fraud:[128]	
	Involving a single mortgage loan	Class H felony
	Involving a pattern of residential mortgage fraud	Class E felony
Article 21: Forgery		
14-119(a)	Forging or counterfeiting bank notes, checks, or securities:	
	Forgery or counterfeiting	Class I felony
	Possession of counterfeit instrument	Class I felony
14-119(b)	Possession of five or more counterfeit instruments	Class G felony

125. G.S. 14-118.5 authorizes a fine up to $500.
126. *See supra* note 125.
127. The maximum fine for this offense is $10,000. A convicted defendant is liable for all taxes, fees, penalties, and interest due to the state resulting from use of the device and must forfeit all profits from its sale or use.
128. The court may order restitution to any person who suffered a financial loss as a result of a violation, and all real and personal property used or derived from a violation is subject to forfeiture as provided in G.S. 14-2.3 and 14-7.20. *See* G.S. 14-118.16.

Statute	Description of Offense	Punishment
14-120	Forged instruments:	
	Uttering forged instrument	Class I felony
	Forging endorsement	Class I felony
	Uttering instrument with forged endorsement	Class I felony
Common law	Common law forgery	Class 1 misdemeanor under 14-3(a)
Common law	Common law uttering of forged paper	Class 1 misdemeanor under 14-3(a)
14-121	Selling forged securities	Class H felony
14-122	Forgery of deeds, wills, etc.	Class H felony
14-122.1	Falsifying documents issued by school or government agency	Class 1 misdemeanor
14-124	Corporate stock certificates:	
	Forgery	Class I felony
	Uttering	Class I felony

Article 22: Damages and Other Offenses to Land and Fixtures

14-127	Injury to real property	Class 1 misdemeanor
14-127.1	Graffiti vandalism	Class 1 misdemeanor[129]
14-128	Injury to trees, crops, lands of another	Class 1 misdemeanor
14-129	Taking certain wild plants from land of another	Class 3 misdemeanor[130]
14-129.2	Taking of sea oats	Class 3 misdemeanor[131]
14-129.3	Taking Venus flytrap	Class H felony
14-130	Trespassing on public lands	Class 1 misdemeanor
14-132(a)(1), (d)	Disorderly conduct in or near public building or facility	Class 2 misdemeanor
14-132(a)(2), (d)	Defacing or injuring public building or facility	Class 2 misdemeanor
14-132(a)(3), (d)	Committing nuisance in or near public building or facility	Class 2 misdemeanor
14-132.2(a)	Injuring public school bus	Class 1 misdemeanor

129. A person convicted of the Class 1 misdemeanor must be fined a minimum of $500 and, if community or intermediate punishment is imposed, must perform 24 hours of community service. G.S. 14-127.1(c) provides that it is a Class H felony if the person had two or more prior convictions of this offense, the current violation was committed after the second conviction, and the current violation resulting in a second conviction was committed after the first violation.

130. G.S. 14-129 provides that the Class 3 misdemeanor is punished only by a fine of not less than $75 nor more than $175 for each offense, with each plant taken constituting a separate offense.

131. This offense is punishable by a fine of not less than $25 nor more than $200.

Statute	Description of Offense	Punishment
14-132.2(b)	Entering public school bus after being forbidden	Class 1 misdemeanor
14-132.2(c)	Refusing to leave public school bus after demand	Class 1 misdemeanor
14-132.2(c1)	Impeding or delaying public school bus	Class 1 misdemeanor
14-134.3(a)	Domestic criminal trespass	Class 1 misdemeanor
14-134.3(b)	Domestic criminal trespass on safe house by person with deadly weapon	Class G felony
14-135	Cutting down, injuring, or removing timber from another's property:	
	Timber valued up to $1,000	Class 1 misdemeanor
	Timber valued more than $1,000	Class H felony
14-136	Setting fire to grass, brushlands, or woodlands:	
	First offense	Class 2 misdemeanor
	Subsequent offense	Class 1 misdemeanor
	With intent to damage property of another	Class I felony
14-137	Setting fire to woods or fields	Class 2 misdemeanor
14-138.1	Starting fire on grassland, brushland, or woodland and failing to extinguish fire	Class 3 misdemeanor[132]
14-140.1	Burning brush, grass, or other material without watchman	Infraction
14-144	Defacing or damaging house, church, fence, or wall:	
	Causing damage of $5,000 or less	Class 2 misdemeanor
	Causing damage of more than $5,000	Class I felony
14-145	Unlawful posting of advertisement	Class 3 misdemeanor
14-148(a)(1), (c)	Throwing trash in cemetery:[133]	
	Causing damage less than $1,000	Class 1 misdemeanor
	Causing damage of $1,000 or more	Class I felony

132. The punishment for this offense may include a fine of not less than $10 nor more than $50.
133. G.S. 14-148(c) provides that the court shall consider, as an alternative to imposition of a fine or jail term, the appropriateness of restitution or reparation as a condition of probation.

Statute	Description of Offense	Punishment
14-148(a)(2), (c)	Vandalizing cemetery enclosure:[134]	
	Causing damage of less than $1,000	Class 1 misdemeanor
	Causing damage of $1,000 or more	Class I felony
14-148(a)(3), (c)	Vandalizing flowers, plants, and other articles in cemetery:[135]	
	Causing damage of less than $1,000	Class 1 misdemeanor
	Causing damage of $1,000 or more	Class I felony
14-149(a)(1)	Vandalizing casket or other repository of human remains	Class I felony
14-149(a)(2)	Vandalizing grave marker or ornament	Class I felony
14-149(a1)	Vandalizing human remains interred in cemetery	Class H felony
14-151	Interfering with gas, electric, and steam appliances, or meters	Class 1 misdemeanor
	Second or subsequent violation	Class H felony for second or subsequent violation
	Significant property damage or public endangerment	Class F felony if significant property damage or public endangerment
	Offense resulting in death	Class D felony if violation results in death of another
14-154	Damaging telegraph, telephone, cable telecommunications, electric power line, or equipment related to wireless communications	Class I felony
14-155	Unauthorized connection with telephone company	Class 3 misdemeanor[136]
14-156	Injuring fixtures or other property of electric power companies	Class 2 misdemeanor
14-158	Interfering with telephone line	Class 2 misdemeanor
14-159.1	Contaminating public water system	Class C felony
14-159.2(a)(1), (b)	Unauthorized entry into animal research facility with intent to disrupt operations, damage facility, release animals, or interfere with care of animals	Class 1 misdemeanor[137]

---

134. *See supra* note 133.
135. *See supra* note 133.
136. Each day's continuance of an unlawful connection is a separate offense.
137. G.S. 14-159.2(c) provides that a violation of G.S. 14-159.2(a) involving release of an animal with an infectious disease is a Class I felony. G.S. 14-159.2(d) provides that, as a condition of probation, the court may order a person convicted under G.S. 14-159.2 to make restitution for damages resulting from the violation, including such costs as replacing animals and equipment.

Statute	Description of Offense	Punishment
14-159.2(a)(2), (b)	Damaging animal research facility	Class 1 misdemeanor[138]
14-159.2(a)(3), (b)	Unauthorized release of animal from animal research facility	Class 1 misdemeanor[139]
14-159.2(a)(4), (b)	Interfering with care of animal in animal research facility	Class 1 misdemeanor[140]
14-159.3	Trespassing with motorized all-terrain vehicle	Class 2 misdemeanor
14-159.4	Willfully tampering with another's property to obtain nonferrous metals:	
	Disrupting critical infrastructure	Class 1 misdemeanor
	Total cost of damages is less than $1,000	Class 1 misdemeanor
	Total cost of damages is $1,000–$9,999	Class H felony
	Total cost of damages is $10,000 or more	Class F felony
	Resulting in serious injury	Class A1 misdemeanor
	Resulting in serious bodily injury	Class F felony
	Resulting in death	Class D felony

Article 22A: Trespassing upon "Posted" Property to Hunt, Fish, Trap, or Remove Pine Needles/Straw

Statute	Description of Offense	Punishment
14-159.6(a)	Hunting or fishing on posted property	Class 2 misdemeanor
14-159.6(b)	Raking or removing pine straw on posted property	Class 1 misdemeanor
14-159.8	Mutilation, etc., of "posted" signs, posting without consent of owner or agent	Class 3 misdemeanor, but punishable only by up to $100 fine

Article 22B: First- and Second-Degree Trespass

Statute	Description of Offense	Punishment
14-159.12(a), (b)	First-degree trespass	Class 2 misdemeanor[141]
14-159.12(c)	First-degree trespass on premises of an electric, water, natural gas utility, or agricultural activities facility	Class A1 misdemeanor
14-159.12(d)	First-degree trespass in violation of 14-159.12(c) with the intent to disrupt facility's operations or involving the risk of serious bodily injury	Class H felony
14-159.12(f)	First-degree trespass when reentry after removal by valid order or writ for possession	Class I felony; mandatory fine of at least $1,000[142]

138. *See supra* note 137.
139. *See supra* note 137.
140. *See supra* note 137.
141. For offenses committed on or after December 1, 2018, this offense includes a trespass on the lands of the Eastern Band of Cherokee Indians by a person who has been excluded by a resolution passed by the Eastern Band of Cherokee Indian Tribal Council. S.L. 2018-66.
142. This offense was enacted by S.L. 2016-26, effective for offenses committed on or after December 1, 2016.

Statute	Description of Offense	Punishment
14-159.12(f)	First-degree trespass under color of title created with false evidence of ownership or possession	Class I felony; mandatory fine of least $1,000[143]
14-159.12(f)	Second or subsequent first-degree trespass on the lands of the Eastern Band of Cherokee Indians	Class I felony; mandatory fine of at least $1,000[144]
14-159.13	Second-degree trespass	Class 3 misdemeanor
Common law	Forcible trespass	Class 1 misdemeanor

Article 22C: Cave Protection Act

14-159.21	Vandalism of cave	Class 3 misdemeanor

Article 23: Trespasses to Personal Property

14-160(a)	Willful injury to personal property, causing damage up to $200	Class 2 misdemeanor
14-160(b)	Willful injury to personal property, causing more than $200 damage	Class 1 misdemeanor
14-160.1	Altering identification marks on personal property	Class 1 misdemeanor
14-160.2(a)	Tampering with permanent number or identification mark on firearm to conceal firearm's identity	Class H felony
14-160.2(b)	Knowingly selling, buying, or possessing any firearm with the permanent number or identification mark altered to conceal firearm's identity	Class H felony
14-160.3	Injuring or interfering with firefighting or emergency medical services vehicle or machinery	Class 1 misdemeanor[145]
14-162	Removing boats	Class 2 misdemeanor
14-163	Poisoning livestock	Class I felony
14-163.1(a1)	Killing law enforcement, assistance, or search and rescue animal	Class H felony
14-163.1(b)	Causing or attempting to cause serious harm to law enforcement, assistance, or search and rescue animal	Class I felony
14-163.1(c)	Causing or attempting to cause harm to law enforcement, assistance, or search and rescue animal	Class 1 misdemeanor
14-163.1(d)	Harassing, delaying, or obstructing, or attempting to delay or obstruct, law enforcement, assistance, or search and rescue animal	Class 2 misdemeanor

143. This offense was enacted by S.L. 2016-26, effective for offenses committed on or after December 1, 2016.
144. This offense was enacted by S.L. 2018-66, effective for offenses committed on or after December 1, 2018.
145. This offense was enacted by S.L. 2017-89, effective for offenses committed on or after December 1, 2017.

Statute	Description of Offense	Punishment
Article 24: Vehicles and Draft Animals—Protection of Bailor against Acts of Bailee		
14-165	Malicious injury to hired personal property	Class 2 misdemeanor
14-167	Failing to return:	
	Rented motor vehicle worth more than $4,000	Class H felony
	Other rented property	Class 3 misdemeanor
14-168	Renting equipment or vehicle with intent to defraud	Class 2 misdemeanor
14-168.1	Conversion by bailee, lessee, tenant, or person with power of attorney:	
	If value of property is $400 or less	Class 3 misdemeanor
	If value of property exceeds $400	Class H felony
14-168.4	Failing to return rented equipment on which there is purchase option, with intent to defeat owner's rights	Class 3 misdemeanor
Article 26: Offenses against Public Morality and Decency		
14-177	Crime against nature	Class I felony
14-178	Incest:[146]	
	With person under 13 by defendant at least 12 and at least 4 years older than person	Class B1 felony
	With person 13, 14, or 15 by defendant at least 6 years older than person	Class B1 felony
	With person 13, 14, or 15 by defendant more than 4 but less than 6 years older than person	Class C felony
	In all other cases	Class F felony
14-183	Bigamy	Class I felony
14-184	Fornication and adultery	Class 2 misdemeanor
14-188	Keeping disorderly or bawdy house	Class 2 misdemeanor
14-190.1	Disseminating obscenity	Class I felony
14-190.4	Coercing acceptance of obscene publication	Class 1 misdemeanor
14-190.5	Preparing obscene photograph, slide, or film for purpose of dissemination	Class 1 misdemeanor
14-190.5A	Disclosure of private images	Class H felony if committed by person 18 or older

146. This offense requires sex offender registration.

Statute	Description of Offense	Punishment
		Class 1 misdemeanor if first offense by person under 18 Class H felony for second or subsequent offense by person under 18
14-190.6	Using person under 16 to assist in obscenity offense	Class I felony [147]
14-190.7	Disseminating obscenity to person under 16	Class I felony
14-190.8	Disseminating obscenity to person under 13	Class I felony
14-190.9(a)	Indecent exposure	Class 2 misdemeanor
14-190.9(a1)	Indecent exposure if defendant is 18 or older, person is under 16, and defendant acts for sexual purpose	Class H felony [148]
14-190.9(a2)	Indecent exposure on private premises to anyone other than consenting adult	Class 2 misdemeanor
14-190.9(a4)	Indecent exposure by person 18 or older in private residence where person is not a resident in presence of another person under 16 who is a resident	Class 2 misdemeanor
14-190.9(a5)	Indecent exposure by person in private place with knowing intent to be seen by person in a public place	Class 2 misdemeanor
14-190.14	Displaying material harmful to minors	Class 2 misdemeanor [149]
14-190.15(a), (d)	Disseminating material harmful to minors	Class 1 misdemeanor
14-190.15(b), (d)	Exhibiting harmful performance to minor	Class 1 misdemeanor
14-190.16	First-degree sexual exploitation of minor	Class C felony [150]
14-190.17	Second-degree sexual exploitation of minor	Class E felony [151]
14-190.17A	Third-degree sexual exploitation of minor	Class H felony [152]
14-196	Harassing phone calls	Class 2 misdemeanor
14-196.3	Cyberstalking	Class 2 misdemeanor
14-202(a)	Peeping into room occupied by other person	Class 1 misdemeanor [153]

147. This offense requires sex offender registration.
148. This offense requires sex offender registration.
149. G.S. 14-190.14(b) provides that each day's violation is a separate offense.
150. This offense requires sex offender registration.
151. This offense requires sex offender registration.
152. This offense requires sex offender registration.
153. The court may require a defendant placed on probation for a first conviction under G.S. 14-202 to obtain a psychological evaluation and to comply with any recommended treatment; if the court places a defendant on probation for a second or subsequent conviction, the court must impose these requirements. *See* G.S. 14-202(j). A person whose image is captured or

Statute	Description of Offense	Punishment
14-202(a1)	Peeping under or through other person's clothing by mirror or other device	Class 1 misdemeanor[154]
14-202(c)	Peeping while possessing device to create photographic image	Class A1 misdemeanor[155]
14-202(d)	Peeping while using device to create photographic image for sexual purpose	Class I felony[156]
14-202(e)	Secretly using device to create photographic image underneath or through other person's clothing	Class I felony[157]
14-202(f)	Secretly installing device in room to create photographic image for sexual purpose	Class I felony[158]
14-202(g)	Possessing photographic image obtained in violation of 14-202	Class I felony[159]
14-202(h)	Disseminating image obtained in violation of 14-202	Class H felony[160]
14-202(i)	Second or subsequent violation of 14-202:[161]	
	Second or subsequent felony	Felony one class higher than felony committed
	Second or subsequent Class A1 misdemeanor	Class I felony
	Second or subsequent Class 1 misdemeanor	Class A1 misdemeanor
14-202.1	Taking, or attempting to take, indecent liberties with child	Class F felony[162]
14-202.2	Indecent liberties between children	Class 1 misdemeanor[163]

---

disseminated in violation of G.S. 14-202 has a civil action for damages as provided in G.S. 14-202(k). G.S. 14-202(l) and G.S. 14-208.6(4)d. provide that if a person is convicted of a violation of subsections (d), (e), (f), (g), or (h) of G.S. 14-202, or a second or subsequent violation of G.S. 14-202(a), (a1), or (c), the sentencing judge may require the person to register as a sex offender under Chapter 14, Article 27A, if the judge rules that the defendant is a danger to the community and requiring registration would further the purposes of Article 27A.

154. *See supra* note 153.
155. *See supra* note 153.
156. *See supra* note 153.
157. *See supra* note 153.
158. *See supra* note 153.
159. *See supra* note 153.
160. *See supra* note 153.
161. *See supra* note 153.
162. This offense requires sex offender registration.
163. This offense occurs when a person under 16 takes or attempts to take indecent liberties with a child who is at least 3 years younger than the person. Because the district court, in its capacity as juvenile court, has exclusive jurisdiction over a person who is under 16 and charged with a misdemeanor, G.S. 14-202.2 only provides the basis for a delinquency petition in juvenile court; the person may not be tried as an adult.

Statute	Description of Offense	Punishment
14-202.3(a), (c)	Soliciting child by computer or other electronic device to commit unlawful sex act:[164]	
	Solicitation	Class H felony
	Solicitation if defendant, or person for whom defendant was arranging meeting, appears at meeting location	Class G felony
14-202.4	Taking or attempting to take indecent liberties with elementary or secondary school student:	
	By teacher, school administrator, student teacher, school safety officer, or coach	Class I felony[165]
	By other school personnel or volunteer if 4 or more years older than student	Class I felony[166]
	By other school personnel or volunteer if less than 4 years older than student	Class I felony[167]
14-202.5	Accessing commercial social networking website by sex offender knowing that site permits minors to become members or maintain personal web pages	Class I felony

Article 26A: Adult Establishments

Statute	Description of Offense	Punishment
14-202.11(a), -202.12	Permitting facility to contain multiple adult establishments:	
	First offense	Class 3 misdemeanor
	Subsequent violation of 14-202.11	Class 2 misdemeanor
	Permitting adult establishment in facility where sexually oriented devices are contained:	
	First offense	Class 3 misdemeanor
	Subsequent violation of 14-202.11	Class 2 misdemeanor
14-202.11(b), -202.12	Permitting multiple occupancy in viewing booth in adult mini-motion picture theater:	
	First offense	Class 3 misdemeanor
	Subsequent violation of 14-202.11	Class 2 misdemeanor

164. This offense requires sex offender registration.
165. This offense requires sex offender registration.
166. This offense requires sex offender registration.
167. This offense is not subject to sex offender registration.

Statute	Description of Offense	Punishment
Article 27: Prostitution[168]		
14-204(a)	Prostitution	Class 1 misdemeanor[169]
14-205.1	Solicitation of prostitution[170]	
	First offense	Class 1 misdemeanor
	Second or subsequent offense	Class H felony
	Person 18 or older solicits person under 18	Class G felony
	Person solicited is severely or profoundly mentally disabled	Class E felony
14-205.2	Patronizing a prostitute	
	First offense	Class A1 misdemeanor
	Second or subsequent offense	Class G felony for second or subsequent offense
	Defendant is 18 or older and prostitute is under 18	Class F felony if defendant is 18 or older and prostitute is under 18[171]
	Prostitute is severely or profoundly mentally disabled	Class D felony if prostitute is severely or profoundly mentally disabled[172]
14-205.3(a), 3(c)	Promoting prostitution	Class F felony, but Class E felony if prior conviction of 14-204, 14-204.1, 14-204.2, or 14-205.3
14-205.3(b)(1), (b)(2), (d)	Promoting prostitution of minor or mentally disabled person by advancing prostitution or profiting from prostitution[173]	Class D felony, but Class C felony if prior conviction of 14-204, 14-204.1, 14-204.2, or 14-205.3
14-205.3(b)(3), (d)	Promoting prostitution of minor or mentally disabled person by confining victim[174]	Class C felony

168. Under G.S. 14-205.4 a court may order a convicted defendant to be examined for a sexually transmitted infection, and if the defendant is placed on probation and is infected, the probation period may begin only with such conditions that will ensure medical treatment. A female defendant may be supervised only by a female probation officer.

169. G.S. 14-204(b) requires probation and a conditional discharge as set out in the subsection. A defendant who is a minor (under 18 years old) is immune from prosecution and is treated as an undisciplined juvenile as set out in the subsection.

170. Punishment for a violation may include participation in a program devised for the education and prevention of sexual exploitation where available. A prayer for judgment continued is prohibited.

171. This offense requires sex offender registration.

172. This offense requires sex offender registration.

173. This offense requires sex offender registration.

174. This offense requires sex offender registration.

Statute	Description of Offense	Punishment
Article 27A: Sex Offender and Public Protection Registration Programs		
14-208.9A(c)	Failing to provide photograph by sex offender on request by sheriff	Class 1 misdemeanor
14-208.11	Violating sex offender registration requirements	Class F felony
14-208.11A	Assisting person who has violated sex offender registration requirements in eluding arrest	Class H felony
14-208.16	Residing near minor by sex offender	Class G felony
14-208.17(a), (c)	Working by sex offender at place where minor is present	Class F felony
14-208.17(b), (c)	Accepting minor into care or custody knowing that sex offender resides at that location	Class F felony
14-208.18	Being on or near location primarily for use of minors by sex offender convicted of certain offenses	Class H felony[175]
14-208.19A	Violation of commercial driver's license restrictions based on required sex offender registration	Class F felony
14-208.44(a)	Failing to enroll by sex offender in satellite monitoring program	Class F felony
14-208.44(b)	Tampering with satellite monitoring device issued to sex offender	Class E felony
14-208.44(c)	Failing to cooperate with Division of Adult Correction guidelines and regulations for satellite monitoring program	Class 1 misdemeanor
Article 28: Perjury		
14-209	Perjury	Class F felony
14-210	Subornation of perjury	Class I felony
Article 29: Bribery		
14-217	Acceptance of bribe by public official, person nominated for office, or person who has filed notice of candidacy	Class F felony
14-218	Offering bribe	Class F felony
14-220	Offering bribe to, or acceptance of bribe by, juror	Class F felony

175. G.S. 115C-390.11 provides that a local school board may expel a student who is subject to G.S. 14-208.18, according to the procedures set out in the statute.

Statute	Description of Offense	Punishment
Article 30: Obstructing Justice		
Common law	Obstruction of justice	Class 1 misdemeanor, but Class H felony if done with deceit and intent to defraud as provided in 14-3
14-221	Breaking or entering jail, or conspiracy to break or enter jail, with intent to injure prisoner	Class F felony
14-221.1	Destruction of evidence	Class I felony
14-221.2	Altering court document or entering unauthorized judgment	Class H felony
14-223	Resisting, delaying, or obstructing officer	Class 2 misdemeanor
14-225(a), (b)	Making false report to law enforcement agency or officer	Class 2 misdemeanor Class H felony if report concerns investigation of disappearance of a child or child victim of Class A, B1, B2, or C felony
14-225.1	Picketing near courthouse with intent to interfere with administration of justice	Class 1 misdemeanor
14-225.2(a)(1), (c)	Harassing juror with intent to influence official action	Class H felony
14-225.2(a)(2), (c)	Harassing juror as result of prior official action	Class I felony
14-226	Intimidating, or attempting to intimidate, witness	Class G felony
14-226.1	Violating certain court orders	Class 3 misdemeanor[176]
14-226.2	Harassment of participant in neighborhood watch program	Class 1 misdemeanor with mandatory minimum $300 fine

176. The punishment for this offense may include a fine up to $250.

Statute	Description of Offense	Punishment
14-226.3(b)	Knowingly interfering with an electronic monitoring device[177]	If committed by a convicted person required to be monitored, it is a felony one class lower than the most serious underlying felony or a misdemeanor one class lower than the most serious underlying misdemeanor, except if the most serious underlying felony is a Class I felony, then the violation is a Class A1 misdemeanor. If committed by a person required to be monitored as a condition of bond or pretrial release, it is a Class 1 misdemeanor. If committed by any other person, it is a Class 2 misdemeanor.
14-226.3(c)	Knowingly soliciting another person to interfere with an electronic monitoring device[178]	See punishment for 14-226.3(b), above

Article 30A: Secret Listening

Statute	Description of Offense	Punishment
14-227.1, -227.3	Listening, or attempting to listen, to conversation between prisoner and attorney by mechanical or electrical device	Class 2 misdemeanor
14-227.2, -227.3	Listening, or attempting to listen, to deliberations of grand or petit jury in criminal case by mechanical or electrical device	Class 2 misdemeanor

Article 31: Misconduct in Public Office

Statute	Description of Offense	Punishment
14-228	Buying or selling public office	Class I felony
14-230	Willful failure by public officer to discharge duties	Class 1 misdemeanor
14-234	Public officer or employees benefiting from public contracts	Class 1 misdemeanor
14-234.1	Misuse of confidential information	Class 1 misdemeanor
14-239	Allowing prisoner to escape	Class 1 misdemeanor
14-242	Failing to return process or making false return	Class 1 misdemeanor

177. G.S. 14-226.3 does not apply to people subject to satellite-based monitoring under North Carolina's sex offender registration and monitoring program, which is governed by G.S. 14-208.44(b), or to juveniles.

178. *See supra* note 177.

Statute	Description of Offense	Punishment
14-247, -251	Private use of public vehicle	Class 2 misdemeanor

Article 32: Misconduct in Private Office

Statute	Description of Offense	Punishment
14-254	Corporate malfeasance	Class H felony

Article 33: Prison Breach and Prisoners

Statute	Description of Offense	Punishment
14-255	Escape while hired out	Class 1 misdemeanor
14-256	Escape from county or municipal facility or officer of such facility	Class 1 misdemeanor
14-256(1)	Escape from county or municipal facility by charged or convicted felon, pending trial or transfer to state prison system	Class H felony
14-256(2)	Escape from county or municipal facility by person serving sentence for felony	Class H felony
14-256.1	Escape from private correctional facility in N.C. by person convicted in another jurisdiction	Class H felony
14-258(a)	Providing forbidden articles or tools for escape:[179]	
	To a prisoner	Class H felony
	When certain violations lead to escape, assault, or insurrection	Class F felony
14-258(c)	Prisoner possessing tools for escape or items to aid in assault or insurrection	Class H felony[180]
14-258.1(a)	Furnishing poison, narcotics, or weapon to inmate	Class H felony[181]
14-258.1(b)	Furnishing alcohol to inmate	Class 1 misdemeanor[182]
14-258.1(c)	Furnishing tobacco or vapor product to state or local confinement facility inmate	Class 1 misdemeanor
14-258.1(d)	Furnishing mobile telephone or wireless communication device to state or local confinement facility inmate or delinquent juvenile confined in youth development center or detention facility	Class H felony
14-258.1(e)	Possession of tobacco or vapor product by local confinement facility inmate	Class 1 misdemeanor[183]

179. S.L. 2018-67, effective for offenses committed on or after December 1, 2018, rewrote this statute.
180. This offense was enacted by S.L. 2018-67, effective for offenses committed on or after December 1, 2018.
181. The subsection provides that if an officer or employee of a state institution or local confinement facility is convicted of this offense, that officer or employee must be dismissed from his or her office or employment.
182. *See supra* note 181.
183. Tobacco and vapor products are prohibited in state correctional facilities under G.S. 148-23.1, although violations are not punished by criminal penalties.

Statute	Description of Offense	Punishment
14-258.1(g)	Possession of mobile telephone or other wireless communication device by state or local confinement facility inmate	Class H felony
14-258.2(a)	Dangerous weapons in prison/jail:	
	Possession of dangerous weapon by inmate	Class H felony
	Assault with dangerous weapon, inflicting bodily injury	Class F felony
	Use of dangerous weapon to effect escape	Class F felony
14-258.2(b)	Use of dangerous weapon to assist escape by inmate	Class H felony
14-258.3	Taking of hostage by prisoner	Class F felony
14-258.4(a)	Malicious conduct by prisoner (throwing or emitting bodily fluids, excrement, or unknown substance by prisoner at government employee)[184]	Class F felony
14-258.4(b)	Malicious conduct by prisoner (exposing genitalia to an employee)	Class I felony[185]
14-259	Aiding escaped prisoner:	
	When prisoner is felon or charged with felony	Class I felony
	When prisoner is misdemeanant or charged with misdemeanor	Class 1 misdemeanor

Article 34: Custodial Institutions

Statute	Description of Offense	Punishment
14-266, -268	Persuading inmate to escape	Class 1 misdemeanor
14-267, -268	Harboring fugitive	Class 1 misdemeanor

Article 35: Offenses against the Public Peace[186]

Statute	Description of Offense	Punishment
14-269(a), -269(c)	Carrying concealed weapon	Class 2 misdemeanor

184. S.L. 2018-67, effective for offenses committed on or after December 1, 2018, added unknown substances to this offense. The same act added a provision, also effective for offenses committed on or after December 1, 2018, requiring sentences imposed under this article to run consecutively to any sentence being served by the person sentenced under this section. That amendment was likely intended to require sentences for malicious conduct by a prisoner to run consecutively to any sentence the defendant may have been serving when the crime was committed, but the wording of the statute leaves it susceptible to different interpretations.

185. This offense was enacted by S.L. 2018-67, effective for offenses committed on or after December 1, 2018. The same act added a provision, also effective for offenses committed on or after December 1, 2018, requiring sentences imposed under this article to run consecutively to any sentence being served by the person sentenced under this section. That amendment was likely intended to require sentences for malicious conduct by a prisoner to run consecutively to any sentence the defendant may have been serving when the crime was committed, but the wording of the statute leaves it susceptible to different interpretations.

186. Upon a conviction of a violation of G.S. 14-269 (carrying concealed weapon), 14-269.7 (possession of handgun by minor), or any other offense involving use of a deadly weapon as defined in G.S. 14-269, the weapon is subject to confiscation and disposition as provided in G.S. 14-269.1.

Statute	Description of Offense	Punishment
14-269(a1), (c)	Carrying concealed pistol or gun:	
	First offense	Class 2 misdemeanor
	Subsequent offense	Class H felony
14-269.2(b)	Firearms on educational property or at school-sponsored activity:	
	Knowingly possessing certain firearms	Class I felony[187]
	Discharging firearm	Class F felony
14-269.2(b1)	Possession of explosive on educational property or at school-sponsored activity	Class G felony[188]
14-269.2(c)	Aiding person under 18 to possess firearm on educational property	Class I felony
14-269.2(c1)	Aiding person under 18 to possess explosive on educational property	Class G felony[189]
14-269.2(d)	Possession of certain weapons or fireworks on educational property	Class 1 misdemeanor
14-269.2(e)	Aiding person under 18 to commit violation of 14-269.2(d)	Class 1 misdemeanor
14-269.3	Carrying gun into public event or establishment serving alcohol	Class 1 misdemeanor
14-269.4	Possession of weapon in courthouse and certain state property	Class 1 misdemeanor
14-269.6	Possession or sale of spring-loaded projectile knife	Class 1 misdemeanor
14-269.7	Willful possession of handgun by person under 18	Class 1 misdemeanor
14-269.8	Possessing, purchasing, or receiving firearm, ammunition, or concealed firearm permit while prohibited by Ch. 50B domestic violence protective order, or attempting to do so	Class H felony
14-275.1	Disorderly conduct at bus or railroad station or airport	Class 3 misdemeanor
14-276.1	Impersonation of firefighter or emergency medical personnel	Class 3 misdemeanor
14-277(a)(1)–(3), (d1)(1)	Impersonation: falsely representing self as law enforcement officer	Class 1 misdemeanor
14-277(a)(4), (d1)(3)	Impersonation: unlawfully operating vehicle with blue light	Class I felony

187. G.S. 14-269.2(f) provides that it is a Class 1 misdemeanor, not a Class I felony, to possess a firearm on educational property if (1) the person is not a student or an employee at the school, (2) the person is not a student or employee at the school attending a curricular or extracurricular activity sponsored by the school, and (3) the firearm is unloaded, is in a motor vehicle, and is in a locked firearm rack or locked container.

188. *See supra* note 79.

189. *See supra* note 79.

Statute	Description of Offense	Punishment
14-277(b)(1)–(4), (d1)(2)	Impersonation: falsely representing self as law enforcement officer and acting as such	Class 1 misdemeanor[190]
14-277(b)(5), (d1)(4)	Impersonation: unlawfully operating vehicle with blue light and causing reasonable person to yield or stop	Class H felony
14-277(e)	Impersonation of city, county, or state employee	Class 1 misdemeanor
14-277.1	Communicating threats	Class 1 misdemeanor
14-277.2	Carrying weapon at parade or demonstration	Class 1 misdemeanor
14-277.3A	Stalking:[191]	
	First offense	Class A1 misdemeanor
	Subsequent offense	Class F felony
	While court order in effect prohibiting conduct described in 14-277.3A	Class H felony
14-277.4(a), (c)	Obstructing health care facility:	
	First offense	Class 2 misdemeanor
	Second conviction within three years of first conviction	Class 1 misdemeanor
	Third or subsequent conviction within three years of most recent conviction	Class I felony
14-277.4(b), (c)	Injuring, or threatening to injure, person obtaining, aiding another to obtain, or providing health care services:	
	First offense	Class 2 misdemeanor
	Second conviction within three years of first conviction	Class 1 misdemeanor
	Third or subsequent conviction within three years of most recent conviction	Class I felony
14-277.4(d)	Violating injunction obtained pursuant to 14-277.4	Criminal contempt, punishable by not less than 30 days or more than one year
14-277.4A(b), -277.4(c)	Targeted picketing of residence	Class 2 misdemeanor
14-277.4A(d)	Violating injunction obtained pursuant to 14-277.4A	Criminal contempt, punishable by not less than 30 days or more than one year

190. G.S. 14-277(d1)(2) provides that the court may impose an intermediate punishment for this offense even when structured sentencing authorizes only a community punishment.

191. G.S. 14-277.3A(d) provides that if a person is convicted of the misdemeanor version of the offense and is sentenced to a community punishment, the court must place the person on supervised probation in addition to any other punishment.

Statute	Description of Offense	Punishment
14-277.5	Making false report concerning mass violence on educational property	Class H felony[192]
14-277.6	Communicating a threat of mass violence on educational property	Class H felony[193]
14-277.7	Communicating a threat of mass violence at a place of religious worship	Class H felony[194]

Article 36: Offenses against the Public Safety

14-280	Shooting or throwing at train	Class I felony
14-280.1	Trespassing on railroad right-of-way	Class 3 misdemeanor
14-280.2	Pointing laser device at aircraft	Class H felony
14-280.3	Interference with manned aircraft by unmanned aircraft systems	Class H felony
14-281.1	Throwing object at sports event	Class 3 misdemeanor
14-283	Exploding dynamite cartridge or bomb	Class 1 misdemeanor
14-284	Unlicensed sale of explosives	Class 1 misdemeanor
14-284.1	Violating regulations governing sale of explosives	Class 2 misdemeanor
14-284.2	Dumping toxic substances	Class F felony[195]
14-286	Giving false fire alarm	Class 2 misdemeanor
14-286.1	Making false ambulance request	Class 3 misdemeanor
14-286.2	Interfering with emergency communication	Class A1 misdemeanor

Article 36A: Riots, Civil Disorders, and Emergencies

Common law	Going armed to the terror of the people	Class 1 misdemeanor
Common law	Unlawful assembly	Class 1 misdemeanor
14-288.2(b)	Engaging in riot	Class 1 misdemeanor
14-288.2(c)(1)	Engaging in riot resulting in more than $1,500 property damage or serious bodily injury	Class H felony

---

192. G.S. 14-277.5(c) authorizes the court to order a person convicted of a violation to pay restitution, including costs and consequential damages resulting from the disruption of normal activity on the premises. For offenses committed on or after December 1, 2018, S.L. 2018-72 adds G.S. 14-277.8, creating a conditional discharge for certain defendants under the age of 20 convicted of this offense.

193. This offense was enacted by S.L. 2018-72, effective for offenses committed on or after December 1, 2018. Under G.S. 14-277.8, certain defendants under the age of 20 convicted of this offense are eligible for a conditional discharge.

194. *See supra* note 193.

195. G.S. 14-284.2 authorizes a fine up to $100,000 per day of violation.

Statute	Description of Offense	Punishment
14-288.2(c)(2)	Engaging in riot while possessing dangerous weapon or substance	Class H felony
14-288.2(d)	Inciting riot	Class 1 misdemeanor
14-288.2(e)	Inciting riot resulting in more than $1,500 property damage or serious bodily injury	Class F felony
14-288.4(a)(1) through (a)(7)	Disorderly conduct	Class 2 misdemeanor
14-288.4(a)(8), (c)	Disorderly conduct at funeral:	
	First offense	Class 1 misdemeanor
	Second offense	Class I felony
	Third or subsequent offense	Class H felony
14-288.5	Failing to disperse when commanded	Class 2 misdemeanor
14-288.6(a)	Trespass during emergency	Class 1 misdemeanor
14-288.6(b)	Looting	Class H felony
14-288.8	Manufacture, sale, possession, etc., of weapon of mass death and destruction	Class F felony
14-288.9	Assault causing physical injury on emergency personnel	Class I felony
	Assault on emergency personnel with dangerous weapon or substance	Class F felony
14-288.20A	Violation of emergency prohibitions and restrictions	Class 2 misdemeanor

Article 36B: Nuclear, Biological, or Chemical Weapons of Mass Destruction

Statute	Description of Offense	Punishment
14-288.21	Manufacture, sale, possession, etc., of nuclear, biological, or chemical weapon of mass destruction	Class B1 felony
14-288.22(a)	Injuring another with weapon in 14-288.21	Class A felony punishable by life imprisonment without parole
14-288.22(b)	Attempt, solicitation, or conspiracy to injure another with weapon in 14-288.21	Class B1 felony
14-288.22(c)	Delivery or attempt to deliver through mail weapon in 14-288.21	Class B1 felony
14-288.23(a)	False report that weapon in 14-288.21 is in any place or structure	Class D felony[196]

196. The court may order a person convicted of this offense to pay restitution for disruption of normal activities.

Statute	Description of Offense	Punishment
14-288.24(a)	Perpetrating hoax regarding weapon in 14-288.21	Class D felony[197]

Article 37: Lotteries, Gaming, Bingo, and Raffles[198]

Statute	Description of Offense	Punishment
14-290	Promoting or conducting unauthorized lottery	Class 2 misdemeanor[199]
14-291	Selling lottery tickets	Class 2 misdemeanor
14-291.1	Selling "numbers" tickets	Class 2 misdemeanor
14-291.2	Pyramid scheme:[200]	
	Establishing or operating	Class H felony
	Participating in or otherwise promoting	Class 2 misdemeanor
14-292	Gambling	Class 2 misdemeanor
14-293	Allowing gambling in houses of entertainment	Class 2 misdemeanor[201]
14-295	Keeping or playing gaming tables, illegal punchboards, and slot machines	Class 2 misdemeanor
14-297	Allowing gaming tables, illegal punchboards, or slot machines on premises	Class 2 misdemeanor
14-301, -303	Operating or possessing slot machine	Class 2 misdemeanor
14-302, -303	Operating or possessing gambling devices	Class 2 misdemeanor
14-304, -309	Manufacture, sale, etc., of slot machine:	
	First offense	Class 1 misdemeanor
	Second offense	Class H felony
	Third or subsequent offense	Class G felony
14-305, -309	Agreeing to provide thing of value to user of slot machine:	
	First offense	Class 1 misdemeanor
	Second offense	Class H felony
	Third or subsequent offense	Class G felony

197. *See supra* note 196.

198. G.S. 14-298 and 14-299 set out various provisions for the seizure, forfeiture, destruction, etc., of property and money for various offenses in Article 37.

199. G.S. 14-290 authorizes a maximum $2,000 fine.

200. G.S. 14-291.2(c) provides that a superior court judge may, on petition of the attorney general or district attorney, enjoin the continuation of a pyramid scheme, assess civil penalties and attorneys' fees in such a proceeding, and appoint a receiver to secure assets obtained by the defendant through his or her participation in the scheme. G.S. 14-291.2(a) provides that any person who participates in or otherwise promotes a pyramid scheme shall be deemed to have participated in a lottery.

201. G.S. 14-293 provides that any person convicted of this offense shall forfeit his or her license to do business and forever be barred from doing any of the businesses set out in the statute.

Statute	Description of Offense	Punishment
14-306(d), -309	Making unlawful payout to player:	
	First offense	Class 1 misdemeanor
	Second offense	Class H felony
	Third or subsequent offense	Class G felony
14-306.1A, -309	Violation of video gaming machine ban:	
	First offense	Class 1 misdemeanor
	Second offense	Class H felony
	Third or subsequent offense	Class G felony
	Offense involving operation of five or more machines	Class G felony
14-306.3(a), -309	Promoting, operating, or conducting server-based electronic game promotion:[202]	
	First offense	Class 1 misdemeanor
	Second offense	Class H felony
	Third or subsequent offense	Class G felony
14-306.3(b), -309	Possession of game terminal for purpose of promoting, operating, or conducting server-based electronic game promotion:[203]	
	First offense	Class 1 misdemeanor
	Second offense	Class H felony
	Third or subsequent offense	Class G felony
	Offense involving possession of five or more machines	Class G felony
14-306.4	Operating an electronic machine to conduct or promote a sweepstakes using an entertaining display:[204]	
	First offense	Class 1 misdemeanor
	Second offense	Class H felony
	Third or subsequent offense	Class G felony
14-309.5	Licensed exempt organization conducting bingo in violation of Part 2, Article 37	Class 2 misdemeanor

202. G.S. 14-298 provides for the seizure and destruction of any game terminal described in G.S. 14-306.3(b); it is unclear whether this provision applies to violations of both G.S. 14-306.3(a) and 14-306.3(b) or only to violations of the latter subsection. G.S. 14-299 provides for the seizure and destruction, sale, or forfeiture of money and other property or things of value exhibited for the purpose of alluring people to bet on any game or used in the conduct of any such game; unlike G.S. 14-298, G.S. 14-299 does not specifically refer to game terminals under G.S. 14-306.3. A conviction of a violation of G.S. 14-306.3 results in automatic revocation of an alcoholic beverage control (ABC) permit under Chapter 18B and contract to sell lottery tickets under Article 5C of Chapter 18C.

203. *See supra* note 202.

204. Each violation of the statute constitutes a separate offense. *See* G.S. 14-306.4(e). The statute does not apply to activities lawfully conducted on Indian lands in accordance with a gaming compact. G.S. 14-306.4(c) provides that the statute prohibits any mechanism that seeks to avoid application of the statute through subterfuge or pretense.

Statute	Description of Offense	Punishment
14-309.5	Operating bingo without license or while license revoked, misapplying bingo moneys, or providing consulting services to licensee	Class I felony
14-309.14(5)	Operating beach bingo without a license	Class 2 misdemeanor[205]
14-309.14(5)	Providing false information in application for beach bingo license	Class 2 misdemeanor[206]
14-309.15(a)	Unlawful raffle	Class 2 misdemeanor[207]
14-309.20	Conducting greyhound racing for monetary remuneration	Class 1 misdemeanor

Article 39: Protection of Minors

Statute	Description of Offense	Punishment
14-313(b)	Sale of tobacco products or cigarette wrapping papers to person under 18:[208]	
	Selling or distributing to person under 18	Class 2 misdemeanor
	Purchasing on behalf of person under 18	Class 2 misdemeanor
	Failing to demand proof of age of person under 18	Class 2 misdemeanor
	Failing to post required notice	Infraction[209]
14-313(b1)	Unlawfully distributing tobacco products through vending machine	Class 2 misdemeanor[210]
14-313(c)	Purchase of tobacco products or cigarette wrapping papers by person under 18:[211]	
	Purchasing, receiving, or attempting to purchase or receive	Class 2 misdemeanor
	Presenting false proof of age	Class 2 misdemeanor
14-313(d)	Sending or assisting person under 18 to purchase or receive tobacco products or cigarette wrapping papers	Class 2 misdemeanor[212]
14-315(a)	Selling or giving weapon other than handgun to person under 18	Class 1 misdemeanor[213]
14-315(a1)	Selling or giving handgun to person under 18	Class H felony[214]

205. This offense was enacted by S.L. 2016-27, effective for offenses committed on or after December 1, 2016.
206. This offense was enacted by S.L. 2016-27, effective for offenses committed on or after December 1, 2016.
207. G.S. 14-309.15(a) provides that a person convicted of this offense may not conduct a raffle for one year.
208. G.S. 14-313(f) provides that any person charged with a misdemeanor shall be qualified for deferred prosecution if he or she has not previously been placed on probation for a violation of G.S. 14-313 and so states under oath.
209. G.S. 14-313(b) provides that a first offense is punishable by a $25 penalty and a subsequent offense by a $75 penalty.
210. *See supra* note 208.
211. *See supra* note 208. It is not unlawful for an employee under 18 to purchase or accept receipt when required in performing his or her duties.
212. *See supra* note 208.
213. G.S. 14-315 provides that the defendant shall forfeit the proceeds of any sale.
214. *See supra* note 213.

Statute	Description of Offense	Punishment
14-315.1	Storing firearm in manner accessible to minor	Class 1 misdemeanor
14-315.2(a), (c)	Failing to provide written copy of 14-315.1 to purchaser of firearm	Class 1 misdemeanor
14-315.2(b), (c)	Failing to post notice warning purchaser of duty to store firearm	Class 1 misdemeanor
14-316	Permitting person under 12 to use dangerous firearm	Class 2 misdemeanor
14-316.1	Contributing to delinquent, undisciplined, abused, or neglected condition of juvenile	Class 1 misdemeanor
14-318	Exposing child under 8 to danger of fire	Class 1 misdemeanor
14-318.2	Misdemeanor child abuse	Class A1 misdemeanor[215]
14-318.4(a)	Felony child abuse by intentionally inflicting serious physical injury on child	Class D felony[216]
14-318.4(a1)	Felony child abuse by committing, permitting, or encouraging prostitution by child	Class D felony[217]
14-318.4(a2)	Felony child abuse by parent or legal guardian committing or allowing commission of sexual act on child	Class D felony[218]
14-318.4(a3)	Felony child abuse by intentionally inflicting serious bodily injury on child	Class B2 felony[219]
14-318.4(a4)	Felony child abuse by willful act or grossly negligent omission resulting in serious bodily injury to child	Class E felony[220]
14-318.4(a5)	Felony child abuse by willful act or grossly negligent omission resulting in serious physical injury to child	Class G felony[221]
14-318.5(b)	Knowing or wanton failure by parent or other person providing care to or supervision of child under 16 to report disappearance of child to law enforcement	Class I felony
14-318.5(c)	Failure of person who reasonably suspects disappearance of child under 16 and reasonably suspects danger to child to report suspicions to law enforcement	Class 1 misdemeanor

215. G.S. 14-318.2 creates three separate offenses: (1) inflicting physical injury on a child, (2) allowing physical injury to be inflicted on a child, and (3) creating or allowing to be created a substantial risk of physical injury to a child. G.S. 14-318.2(c) provides that a parent who voluntarily relinquishes an infant less than 7 days of age pursuant to G.S. 14-322.3 may not be prosecuted for this offense for acts or omissions relating to the care of that infant.

216. G.S. 14-318.4(c) provides that voluntary relinquishment of an infant less than 7 days of age pursuant to G.S. 14-322.3 may be treated as a mitigating factor at sentencing for a violation of G.S. 14-318.4 involving that infant.

217. *See supra* note 213. This offense requires sex offender registration.

218. *See supra* note 213. This offense requires sex offender registration.

219. *See supra* note 216.

220. *See supra* note 216.

221. *See supra* note 216.

Statute	Description of Offense	Punishment
14-320.1	Transporting child outside state with intent to violate custody order	Class I felony
14-321.1	Baby sitting by or near sex offender:	
	First offense	Class 1 misdemeanor
	Subsequent offense	Class H felony
14-321.2(a), (c)	Unlawful transfer of custody of minor child	Class A1 misdemeanor[222]
14-321.2(a), (d)	Unlawful transfer of custody of minor child resulting in serious injury to child	Class G felony[223]

Article 40: Protection of the Family[224]

Statute	Description of Offense	Punishment
14-322(b), (f)	Abandonment of spouse without providing adequate support:[225]	
	First offense	Class 2 misdemeanor
	Subsequent offense under 14-322	Class 1 misdemeanor
14-322(c), (f)	Failing to provide adequate support while living with dependent spouse:[226]	
	First offense	Class 2 misdemeanor
	Subsequent offense under 14-322	Class 1 misdemeanor
14-322(d), (f)	Nonsupport of child by parent:[227]	
	First offense	Class 2 misdemeanor
	Subsequent offense under 14-322	Class 1 misdemeanor
14-322.1	Abandonment of child for six months and failure to support	Class I felony
14-326.1	Failing to support parent:	
	First offense	Class 2 misdemeanor
	Subsequent offense	Class 1 misdemeanor

Article 44: Regulation of Sales

Statute	Description of Offense	Punishment
14-344	Ticket scalping	Class 2 misdemeanor

222. This offense was enacted by S.L. 2016-115, effective for offenses committed on or after December 1, 2016.
223. *See supra* note 222.
224. A parent who voluntarily relinquishes an infant less than 7 days of age pursuant to G.S. 14-322.3 may not be prosecuted under G.S. 14-322 or G.S. 14-322.1 for abandonment or nonsupport of that infant. *See* G.S. 14-322.3.
225. In addition to imposing the authorized punishment for this offense, the court is authorized to enter an order for support. *See* G.S. 14-322(e).
226. *See supra* note 225.
227. *See supra* note 225.

Statute	Description of Offense	Punishment
14-344.1, -344	Internet sale of ticket that does not comply with requirements of 14-344.1	Class 2 misdemeanor

Article 47: Cruelty to Animals

Statute	Description of Offense	Punishment
14-360(a)	Intentional cruelty to animals	Class 1 misdemeanor
14-360(a1)	Killing animal by starvation	Class H felony
14-360(b)	Malicious cruelty to animals	Class H felony[228]
14-361	Instigating or promoting cruelty to animals	Class 1 misdemeanor
14-361.1	Abandonment of animals without justifiable excuse	Class 2 misdemeanor
14-362	Cock fighting	Class I felony[229]
14-362.1(a)	Promoting fighting or baiting of animals other than cocks or dogs	Class 2 misdemeanor[230]
14-362.1(b)	Possessing or training of animal other than cock or dog with intent to use in fighting exhibition	Class 2 misdemeanor
14-362.1(c)	Participating as spectator at animal fight other than cock or dog fight	Class 2 misdemeanor
14-362.1(d)	Violation of 14-362.1(a) within three years of prior conviction	Class I felony
14-362.2(a)	Promoting fighting or baiting of dog	Class H felony[231]
14-362.2(b)	Possessing or training dog with intent to use in fighting exhibition	Class H felony[232]
14-362.2(c)	Participating as spectator at dog fight	Class H felony[233]
14-362.3	Maliciously restraining dog with chain or wire grossly in excess of size necessary	Class 1 misdemeanor
14-363	Conveying animal in cruel manner	Class 1 misdemeanor

---

228. This subsection states that it does not increase the punishment for cock fighting under G.S. 14-362 (a Class I felony).

229. G.S. 14-362 provides that a lessor of property who knows that the property is used or intended to be used for fighting or baiting of an animal is under a duty to evict the lessee immediately.

230. G.S. 14-362.1(a) provides that a lessor of property who knows that the property is used or intended to be used for fighting or baiting of an animal is under a duty to evict the lessee immediately.

231. G.S. 14-362.2(a) provides that a lessor of property who knows that the property is used or intended to be used for fighting or baiting of an animal is under a duty to evict the lessee immediately. G.S. 19A-70 provides for a procedure for the court to order a defendant charged with illegally using dogs for fighting to deposit with the clerk of court the expected costs of caring for the dogs pending disposition of the charges. These provisions cover violations of any provision of Chapter 14, Article 47 (the animal cruelty statutes), and G.S. 67-4.3 (attack by dangerous dog).

232. G.S. 19A-70 provides for a procedure for the court to order a defendant charged with illegally using dogs for fighting to deposit with the clerk of court the expected costs of caring for the dogs pending disposition of the charges. These provisions cover violations of any provision of Chapter 14, Article 47 (the animal cruelty statutes), and G.S. 67-4.3 (attack by dangerous dog).

233. *See supra* note 232.

Statute	Description of Offense	Punishment

Article 52: Miscellaneous Police Regulations

14-394	Sending anonymous or threatening letters	Class 1 misdemeanor
14-395.1	Sexual harassment in leasing of property	Class 2 misdemeanor
14-399(c), (a)	Intentional or reckless littering of not more than 15 pounds	Class 3 misdemeanor[234]
14-399(c1), (a1)	Littering of not more than 15 pounds	Infraction[235]
14-399(d), (a)	Intentional or reckless littering of more than 15 pounds but not exceeding 500 pounds	Class 3 misdemeanor[236]
14-399(d1), (a1)	Littering of more than 15 pounds but not exceeding 500 pounds	Infraction[237]
14-399(e), (a)	Intentional or reckless littering of more than 500 pounds or any quantity for commercial purposes, or littering of hazardous waste	Class I felony[238]
14-399(e1), (a1)	Littering of more than 500 pounds	Infraction[239]

234. G.S. 14-399(c) provides that a first offense is punishable by a fine of $250 to $1,000 and that a second offense within three years of a violation of G.S. 14-399(a) is punishable by a fine of $500 to $2,000. A sentence of imprisonment is not authorized, but for a first offense the court may require 8 to 24 hours of community service involving picking up litter or commensurate labor, and for a second offense within three years of a violation of G.S. 14-399(a) the court may require 16 to 50 hours of such community service. G.S. 14-399(f1) provides that a person found guilty of a violation of G.S. 14-399(a) while operating a motor vehicle shall receive one driver's license point under G.S. 20-16(c).

235. G.S. 14-399(c1) provides that a first offense is punishable by a penalty up to $100 and that a subsequent offense within three years of a violation of G.S. 14-399(a1) is punishable by a penalty up to $200. A sentence of imprisonment is not authorized, but for a first offense the court may require 4 to 12 hours of community service involving picking up litter or commensurate labor, and for a subsequent offense within three years of a violation of G.S. 14-399(a1) the court may require 8 to 24 hours of such community service. G.S. 14-399(e2) further provides that if the violation involves littering for commercial purposes or littering of hazardous waste, the court shall order the violator to remove or render harmless the litter, repair or restore property damaged by the litter or pay damages, or perform community service relating to litter.

236. G.S. 14-399(d) provides that an offense is punishable by a fine of $500 to $2,000. A sentence of imprisonment is not authorized, but the court shall require 24 to 100 hours of community service involving picking up litter or commensurate labor. G.S. 14-399(e2) further provides that the court shall order the violator to remove or render harmless the litter, repair or restore property damaged by the litter or pay damages, or perform community service relating to litter. G.S. 14-399(f1) provides that a person found guilty of a violation of G.S. 14-399(a) while operating a motor vehicle shall receive one driver's license point under G.S. 20-16(c).

237. G.S. 14-399(d1) provides that an offense is punishable by a penalty up to $200. A sentence of imprisonment is not authorized, but the court may require 8 to 24 hours of community service involving picking up litter or commensurate labor. G.S. 14-399(e2) further provides that the court shall order the violator to remove the litter or render it harmless, repair or restore damaged property or pay damages, or perform community service relating to litter.

238. G.S. 14-399(e2) provides that the court shall order the violator to remove or render harmless the litter, repair or restore property damaged by the litter or pay damages, or perform community service relating to litter. G.S. 14-399(f1) provides that a person found guilty of a violation of G.S. 14-399(a) while operating a motor vehicle shall receive one driver's license point under G.S. 20-16(c). G.S. 14-399(g) provides that a motor vehicle, vessel, or other machinery involved in the disposal of more than 500 pounds of litter in violation of G.S. 14-399(a) is subject to forfeiture. G.S. 14-399(h) provides that in a civil suit for damages, the court shall order the violator to pay treble damages or $200, whichever is greater, plus the injured party's court costs and attorneys' fees.

239. G.S. 14-399(e1) provides that an offense is punishable by a penalty up to $300. A sentence of imprisonment is not authorized, but the court may require 16 to 50 hours of community service involving picking up litter or commensurate labor. G.S. 14-399(e2) further provides that the court shall order the violator to remove the litter or render it harmless, repair or restore damaged property or pay damages, or perform community service relating to litter.

Statute	Description of Offense	Punishment
14-400(a)	Tattooing of person under 18	Class 2 misdemeanor
14-400(b)	Body piercing of person under 18	Class 2 misdemeanor
14-401	Putting poisonous food or antifreeze in public place	Class 1 misdemeanor
14-401.4	Removing identifying marks on machines and apparatus	Class 1 misdemeanor
14-401.6	Possession, use, or sale of tear gas	Class 2 misdemeanor
14-401.14(a)	Ethnic intimidation	Class 1 misdemeanor
14-401.14(b)	Teaching any technique to be used for ethnic intimidation	Class 1 misdemeanor
14-401.15	Telephone sales recovery services:	
	Engaging in	Class 1 misdemeanor
	Collecting money for	Class H felony
14-401.16(a), (c)	Contaminating food or drink to render person incapacitated or helpless	Class H felony[240]
14-401.16(b), (c)	Manufacture, sale, or delivery of controlled substance, or possession with intent to manufacture, sell, or deliver, for purpose of violating 14-401.16(a)	Class H felony[241]
14-401.17	Removing electronic dog collar:	
	First offense	Class 3 misdemeanor
	Subsequent offense	Class 2 misdemeanor
14-401.18	Sale of packages of cigarettes in violation of federal law	Class A1 misdemeanor
14-401.18A	Sale of certain e-liquid containers (electronic cigarettes) prohibited	Class A1 misdemeanor
14-401.19	Filing false security agreement under UCC	Class I felony
14-401.20	Defrauding drug or alcohol screening test:	
	First offense	Class 1 misdemeanor
	Subsequent offense	Class I felony
14-401.21	Practicing rebirthing technique:	
	First offense	Class A1 misdemeanor
	Subsequent offense	Class I felony
14-401.22(a)	Failing to notify law enforcement of person's death or secretly disposing of body with intent to conceal death	Class I felony[242]

240. G.S. 14-401.16(c) makes this offense a Class G felony if the person acted with the intent of committing an offense under G.S. 14-27.3 (second-degree rape) or G.S. 14-27.5 (second-degree sex offense).

241. *See supra* note 240.

242. It is a Class D felony if a person violates G.S. 14-401.22(a) knowing or having reason to know that the body or human remains are of a person who did not die of natural causes.

Statute	Description of Offense	Punishment
14-401.22(a1)	Failing to notify law enforcement of death of child under 16 or secretly disposing of dead child's body	Class H felony[243]
14-401.22(b)	Aiding or abetting concealing of death of person	Class A1 misdemeanor
14-401.22(c)	Human remains:	
	Willfully disturbing	Class I felony
	Committing or attempting to commit a sexual act upon	Class I felony
14-401.22(d)	Attempting to conceal evidence of death by knowingly tampering with human remains	Class H felony[244]
14-401.23	Manufacture, sale, delivery, possession, or possession with intent to manufacture, sell, or deliver Salvia divinorum or Salvinorin A:	
	First or second offense	Infraction[245]
	Third or subsequent offense	Class 3 misdemeanor
14-401.24	Unlawful possession and use of unmanned aircraft systems:	
	Using unmanned aircraft with weapon attached	Class E felony
	Fish or hunt using unmanned aircraft	Class 1 misdemeanor
14-401.25	Disseminating images taken with technology attached to unmanned aircraft system	Class A1 misdemeanor

Article 52A: Sale of Weapons in Certain Counties[246]

Statute	Description of Offense	Punishment
14-402(a)	Pistols:	
	Sale, transfer, purchase, or receipt without permit	Class 2 misdemeanor
	Receipt through mail without permit	Class 2 misdemeanor
14-404(h)	Failing to surrender permit after notice of revocation by sheriff	Class 2 misdemeanor
14-406, -408	Failure of dealer in pistols and other weapons to keep accurate record of sales	Class 2 misdemeanor

243. It is a Class D felony if a person violates G.S. 14-401.22(a1) knowing or having reason to know that the body or human remains are of a person who did not die of natural causes.

244. It is a Class D felony if a person violates G.S. 14-401.22(d) knowing or having reason to know that the body or human remains are of a person who did not die of natural causes.

245. A first or second offense of G.S. 14-401.23 is punishable by a penalty of not less than $25. *See* G.S. 14-401.23(c)(1).

246. Although the title of Article 52A states that it applies to certain counties, the article appears to apply statewide. *See* John Rubin, *1995 Legislation Affecting Criminal Law and Procedure*, ADMINISTRATION OF JUSTICE BULLETIN 95/03, at 4 (Institute of Government, Sept. 1995), www.sog.unc.edu/sites/www.sog.unc.edu/files/reports/aojb9503_0.pdf (in repealing Article 53 of Chapter 14, which authorized clerks of court to issue weapon permits in certain counties, the General Assembly gave sheriffs sole responsibility for issuing permits under Article 52A). *But see* the commentary to G.S. 14-402 (stating that Article 52A does not apply to Warren or Watauga counties).

Statute	Description of Offense	Punishment
14-408.1(b)	Knowingly soliciting a licensed or private seller to transfer a firearm or ammunition in manner known to violate the law	Class F felony[247]
14-408.1(c)	Providing false information to licensed or private seller of firearms or ammunition with intent to deceive	Class F felony[248]
14-409	Sale or possession of machine gun	Class I felony

Article 54: Sale, etc., of Pyrotechnics

Statute	Description of Offense	Punishment
14-410(a), -415	Making, selling, or using certain fireworks	Class 2 misdemeanor[249]
14-410(b), -415	Selling certain pyrotechnics to person under 16	Class 2 misdemeanor

Article 54A: The Felony Firearms Act

Statute	Description of Offense	Punishment
14-415.1	Possession of firearm by felon	Class G felony
14-415.3	Possession of firearm by person acquitted by reason of insanity or found without capacity to proceed	Class H felony[250]
14-415.4(l)	Knowingly submitting false information in petition to restore firearm rights	Class 1 misdemeanor[251]

Article 54B: Concealed Handgun Permit

Statute	Description of Offense	Punishment
14-415.21(a)	Carrying concealed handgun after having been issued valid permit and failing to carry permit or failing to make required disclosures to law enforcement officer	Infraction[252]
14-415.21(a)	Carrying concealed handgun after having been issued valid permit on private premises where notice that carrying concealed handgun is prohibited by posting notice or by statement of person in legal possession or control of premises	Infraction[253]
14-415.21(a1)	Carrying concealed handgun after having been issued valid permit and carrying concealed handgun in violation of 14-415.11(c)(8) (private premises where concealed handgun prohibited) or 14-415.21(c2) (alcohol or controlled substances ban)	Class 1 misdemeanor
14-415.21	Violation of Article 54B other than violation covered by 14-415.21(a) or 14-415.21(a1)	Class 2 misdemeanor

---

247. A person who induces another to engage in conduct prohibited by G.S. 14-408.1 is accountable as a principal. *See* G.S. 14-408.1(d).
248. *See supra* note 247.
249. A pyrotechnics violation involving an indoor exhibition is a Class 1 misdemeanor. *See* G.S. 14-415.
250. Any weapon seized for a violation of G.S. 14-415.3 must be forfeited to the state.
251. A person convicted under G.S. 14-415.4(l) is permanently prohibited from petitioning to restore his or her firearms rights.
252. A violation of G.S. 14-269(a1) that is also punishable under G.S. 14-415.21(a) is not punishable under G.S. 14-269.
253. The penalty may include a fine up to $500.

Statute	Description of Offense	Punishment
14-415.26(d)	Intentional misrepresentation by applicant, or person assisting applicant for certification, to carry concealed handgun	Class 2 misdemeanor[254]

Article 55: Regulation of Certain Reptiles

14-422(a)	Violation of any provision of Article 55	Class 2 misdemeanor
14-422(b)	Person suffers life-threatening injury or is killed as a result of violation of Article 55 by owner of reptile	Class A1 misdemeanor
14-422(c)	Intentionally releasing into wild nonvenomous reptile, large constricting snake, or crocodilian	Class A1 misdemeanor

Article 58: Records, Tapes, and Other Recorded Devices

14-433, -437	Recording live performances or recorded sounds and distribution of such recordings	Class 1 misdemeanor[255]

Article 58A: Audiovisual Recordings

14-440.1(a1)	Pirating movie in theater by photographic camera to record or transmit not greater than one image	Class 1 misdemeanor
14-440.1(b), (c)	Pirating movie in theater by video camera:[256]	
	First offense	Class I felony with minimum $2,500 fine
	Subsequent offense	Class I felony with minimum $5,000 fine

Article 59: Public Intoxication

14-444	Intoxicated and disruptive in public	Class 3 misdemeanor[257]

254. A violation results in the immediate revocation of the certification to carry a concealed handgun and renders the person ineligible for certification and a concealed handgun permit.

255. It is a Class I felony with a maximum $150,000 fine if the offense (1) involves at least 100 unauthorized articles during any 180-day period or (2) is a third or subsequent conviction of an offense involving at least 26 unauthorized articles during any 180-day period. A conviction of any violation of Article 58A requires the forfeiture and destruction of the infringing articles and devices used in their manufacture.

256. Upon a conviction of a violation of G.S. 14-440.1(b), the court must order the forfeiture and destruction of unauthorized recordings and devices used in connection with the offense.

257. G.S. 14-444(b) provides that a magistrate may not accept a guilty plea and enter judgment for this offense, despite the provisions of G.S. 7A-273(1).

Statute	Description of Offense	Punishment
Article 60: Computer-Related Crime		
14-454(a)	Accessing of computer to defraud or obtain property by false pretenses:	
	When loss or damage exceeds $1,000	Class G felony
	When loss or damage is $1,000 or less	Class 1 misdemeanor
14-454(b)	Unauthorized accessing of computer for purpose other than in 14-454(a)	Class 1 misdemeanor
14-454.1(a)	Accessing of government computer to defraud or obtain property by false pretenses	Class F felony
14-454.1(b)	Accessing of government computer for purpose other than in 14-454.1(a)	Class H felony
14-454.1(c)	Accessing of educational testing materials or scores in government computer	Class 1 misdemeanor
14-455(a)	Damaging computer:	
	When damage exceeds $1,000	Class G felony
	When damage is $1,000 or less	Class 1 misdemeanor
14-455(a1)	Damaging government computer	Class F felony
14-456	Denying computer services to authorized user	Class 1 misdemeanor
14-456.1	Denying government computer services to authorized user	Class H felony
14-457	Threatening to damage computer or computer program with intent to extort	Class H felony
14-458	Computer trespass:	
	Resulting in property damage of $2,500 or more	Class I felony
	Resulting in property damage of less than $2,500	Class 1 misdemeanor
	Resulting in no property damage	Class 3 misdemeanor
14-458.1(a), (b)	Cyberbullying:[258]	
	When defendant is 18 or older at time of offense	Class 1 misdemeanor
	When defendant is under 18 at time of offense	Class 2 misdemeanor
14-458.2(b), (c)	Cyberbullying of school employee by a student	Class 2 misdemeanor[259]

258. A defendant convicted under G.S. 14-458.1(c) is eligible for discharge, dismissal, and expunction of an offense committed before the defendant turned 18.

259. A defendant is eligible for discharge, dismissal, and expunction of an offense committed before the defendant turned 18. *See* G.S. 14-458.2(d). A juvenile may enter into a diversion contract under G.S. 7B-1706. *See* G.S. 14-458.2(e). Unless the superintendent decides otherwise, a student convicted under G.S. 14-458.2 must be transferred, pursuant to G.S. 115C-366.4, to

Statute	Description of Offense	Punishment
Article 61: Trains and Railroads		
14-460	Riding on train unlawfully	Class 3 misdemeanor
14-461	Unauthorized manufacture or sale of switch-lock keys	Class 1 misdemeanor

Chapter 15A: Criminal Procedure Act

Statute	Description of Offense	Punishment
Article 13: DNA Database and Databank		
15A-268(i)	Knowingly tampering with evidence preserved under 15A-268:	
	When evidence is for noncapital case	Class I felony
	When evidence is for first-degree murder case	Class H felony
Article 16: Electronic Surveillance[260]		
15A-287(a)(1)	Unauthorized interception of communication	Class H felony
15A-287(a)(2)	Unauthorized use of device to intercept oral communication	Class H felony
15A-287(a)(3)	Disclosure of unlawfully intercepted communication	Class H felony
15A-287(a)(4)	Use of unlawfully intercepted communication	Class H felony
Article 16B: Use of Unmanned Aircraft Systems		
15A-300.3(c)	Use of an unmanned aircraft system near a confinement or correctional facility:[261]	
	To deliver or attempt to deliver a weapon	Class H felony, with a fine of $1,500
	To deliver or attempt to deliver contraband	Class I felony, with a fine of $1,000
	For any other purpose	Class 1 misdemeanor, with a fine of $500
Article 26: Bail		
15A-543(b)(1)	Failing to appear after release in connection with felony	Class I felony
15A-543(b)(2)	Failing to appear after release following conviction in superior court	Class I felony

another school in the local school administrative unit. If no other school is appropriate, the student must be transferred to a different class or teacher.

260. G.S. 15A-287(g) provides that a public officer who violates G.S. 15A-287(a) shall be removed from and shall be ineligible to hold any public office, elective or appointed.

261. This offense was added by S.L. 2017-179, effective for offenses committed on or after December 1, 2017.

Statute	Description of Offense	Punishment
15A-543(c)	Failing to appear after release in connection with misdemeanor	Class 2 misdemeanor

Article 48: Discovery in the Superior Court

Statute	Description of Offense	Punishment
15A-903(d)	Discovery violations:	
	Pursuant to 15A-903(a)(1)	Class H felony
	Pursuant to 15A-903(c)	Class H felony
	Pursuant to any other provision in 15A-903	Class 1 misdemeanor

Article 81D: Permanent No Contact Order against Convicted Sex Offender

Statute	Description of Offense	Punishment
15A-1340.50(g)	Convicted sex offender knowingly violating a permanent no contact order	Class A1 misdemeanor

Chapter 15C: Address Confidentiality Program

Statute	Description of Offense	Punishment
15C-9(f)	Disclosing information in violation of Chapter 15C	Class 1 misdemeanor[262]

Chapter 18B: Regulation of Alcoholic Beverages[263]

Statute	Description of Offense	Punishment
18B-102	Manufacture, sale, transport, import, delivery, furnishing, purchase, consumption, or possession of alcoholic beverages except as authorized by Chapter 18B	Class 1 misdemeanor
18B-102(a1)	Manufacture, sell, transport, import, deliver, furnish, purchase, consume, or possess powdered alcohol	Class 1 misdemeanor
18B-111, -102(b)	Possession, transportation, or sale of nontaxpaid alcoholic beverage	Class 1 misdemeanor[264]
18B-300(a1), -102(b)	Consumption on premises during time of permit revocation or suspension	Class 1 misdemeanor
18B-300(b), -102(b)	Consumption of wine or beer on premises having only off-premises permit	Class 1 misdemeanor

262. A person convicted of this offense must be assessed a fine of not more than $2,500.

263. G.S. 18B-102(b) provides that a violation of Chapter 18B is a Class 1 misdemeanor "[u]nless a different punishment is otherwise expressly stated." G.S. 18B-102(b) provides that in addition to any fine and sentence of imprisonment, the court may impose the provisions of G.S. 18B-202 (removal from office or discharge from employment of any commission or local board member or employee or ALE agent convicted of violation of Chapter 18B; also restricts contracting abilities of convicted individuals), 18B-503 (sale or destruction of seized beverages), 18B-504 (forfeiture of property connected to offense), and 18B-505 (restitution to law enforcement agency for expenses incurred in purchasing beverages as part of investigation). G.S. 18B-104 authorizes certain administrative penalties for violation of the alcoholic beverage control (ABC) laws by a permittee.

264. The DMV has the discretionary authority to revoke a defendant's driver's license for up to six months under G.S. 20-16(a)(8) for a conviction of illegal transportation of alcoholic beverages.

Statute	Description of Offense	Punishment
18B-301(f)(1), -102(b)	Consumption of fortified wine, spirituous liquor, or mixed beverage on ABC store premises, local board property, or public road or sidewalk[265]	Class 1 misdemeanor
18B-301(f)(2), -102(b)	Displaying fortified wine, spirituous liquor, or mixed beverage at athletic contest	Class 1 misdemeanor
18B-301(f)(4), -102(b)	Possession or consumption of fortified wine, spirituous liquor, or mixed beverage on unauthorized premises	Class 1 misdemeanor
18B-301(f)(7), -102(b)	Possession or consumption of beer or wine on school property of local board of education	Class 1 misdemeanor
18B-302(a), -302.1(a)	Sale of alcoholic beverage to person under 21	Class 1 misdemeanor[266]
18B-302(a1), -302.1(a)	Giving alcoholic beverage to person under 21	Class 1 misdemeanor[267]
18B-302(b)(1), (i), -102(b)	Purchase, attempted purchase, or possession of beer or unfortified wine:[268]	
	By person 19 or 20 years old	Class 3 misdemeanor
	By person under 19	Class 1 misdemeanor
18B-302(b)(2), -102(b)	Purchase, attempted purchase, or possession of fortified wine, spirituous liquor, or mixed beverage by person under 21	Class 1 misdemeanor[269]
18B-302(b)(3), (i), -102(b)	Consumption of alcoholic beverage:[270]	
	By person 19 or 20	Class 3 misdemeanor
	By person under 19	Class 1 misdemeanor
18B-302(c)(1)	Aiding violation of 18B-302(a), (a1), or (b) if aider is under 21	Class 2 misdemeanor[271]

265. S.L. 2017-87, effective June 30, 2017, amended this offense to exempt authorized consumer tasting events.

266. If the court does not impose an active punishment, it must impose at least a $250 fine and 25 hours of community service for a first violation and at least a $500 fine and 150 hours of community service for a subsequent violation within four years of a previous conviction. G.S. 18B-302.2 provides that a person under 21 shall not be prosecuted for a violation of G.S. 18B-302 for possessing or consuming alcoholic beverages if law enforcement becomes aware of the possession or consumption of alcohol by the person solely because the person was seeking medical assistance on behalf of another.

267. *See supra* note 266. A conviction of this offense results in a mandatory one-year DMV driver's license revocation under G.S. 18B-302(g) and G.S. 20-17.3. A defendant must surrender his or her driver's license to the court as required by G.S. 20-24(a).

268. A conviction of this offense, if it involves purchase or attempted purchase, results in a one-year revocation of the person's driver's license under G.S. 18B-302(g) and G.S. 20-17.3. If the offense involves possession, G.S. 15A-145 allows expunction of the conviction in certain circumstances. See *supra* note 266 for the immunity provision in G.S. 18B-302.2.

269. A conviction of this offense, if it involves purchase or attempted purchase, results in a mandatory one-year revocation of the person's driver's license under G.S. 18B-302(g) and G.S. 20-17.3. A defendant must surrender his or her driver's license to the court as required by G.S. 20-24(a). See *supra* note 266 for the immunity provision in G.S. 18B-302.2.

270. *See supra* note 266 for the immunity provision in G.S. 18B-302.2.

271. *See supra* note 266 for the immunity provision in G.S. 18B-302.2. G.S. 20-17.3 requires DMV to revoke for one year the driver's license of a person convicted of violating G.S. 18B-302(c). G.S. 18B-302(c) in turn makes it unlawful to aid or abet another in a violation of G.S. 18B-302(a), (a1), or (b). G.S. 18B-302(g) requires the court to file a conviction report with DMV if the person is convicted of a violation of G.S. 18B-302(a1), 18B-302(b) (but only if the violation occurred while the person was purchasing or attempting to purchase an alcoholic beverage), or 18B-302(c), (e), or (f). Thus, it appears that a person's license may be revoked for aiding and abetting the gift to or purchase of alcoholic beverages by an underage person, but it may not be

Statute	Description of Offense	Punishment
18B-302(c)(2), -302.1(b)	Aiding violation of 18B-302(a), (a1), or (b) if aider is 21 or older	Class 1 misdemeanor[272]
18B-302(e), -102(b)	Fraudulent use of identification:[273]	
	To enter or attempt to enter place where alcoholic beverages are sold or consumed	Class 1 misdemeanor
	To obtain or attempt to obtain alcoholic beverage	Class 1 misdemeanor
	To obtain or attempt to obtain permission to purchase alcoholic beverages	Class 1 misdemeanor
18B-302(f), -102(b)	Allowing use of identification by person who violates or attempts to violate 18B-302(b)	Class 1 misdemeanor[274]
18B-303, -102(b)	Purchase or sale of alcoholic beverage in amount greater than authorized by statute	Class 1 misdemeanor
18B-304, -102(b)	Sale of alcoholic beverage without permit	Class 1 misdemeanor
18B-305(a), -102(b)	Selling or giving alcoholic beverage to intoxicated person by permittee or ABC store employee	Class 1 misdemeanor
18B-307, -102(b)	Manufacture of alcoholic beverage without permit:	
	First offense	Class 1 misdemeanor
	Subsequent offense	Class I felony
18B-401(a)	Transportation of alcoholic beverage:	
	Transportation of open bottle of fortified wine or spirituous liquor in passenger area	Class 3 misdemeanor[275]
	Consumption of beer or unfortified wine by driver of motor vehicle	Class 3 misdemeanor
18B-403.1(a), -303(b), -102(b)	Failure of purchaser to obtain purchase-transportation permit for keg of malt beverage	Class 1 misdemeanor

revoked for the sale of alcoholic beverages to an underage person (prohibited by G.S. 18B-302(a)) or the consumption of alcoholic beverages by an underage person (prohibited by G.S. 18B-302(b)(3)). A defendant subject to one of these mandatory revocations must surrender his or her driver's license to the court as required by G.S. 20-24(a).

272. If the court does not impose an active punishment, it must impose at least a $500 fine and 25 hours of community service for a first violation and at least a $1,000 fine and 150 hours of community service for a subsequent violation within four years of a previous conviction. *See supra* note 266 for the immunity provision in G.S. 18B-302.2. A conviction of this offense results in a one-year mandatory DMV driver's license revocation under G.S. 18B-302(g) and G.S. 20-17.3. The defendant must surrender his or her driver's license to the court as required by G.S. 20-24(a).

273. *See supra* note 266 for the immunity provision in G.S. 18B-302.2. A conviction of this offense results in a mandatory one-year DMV driver's license revocation under G.S. 18B-302(g) and G.S. 20-17.3. The defendant must surrender his or her driver's license to the court as required by G.S. 20-24(a).

274. *See supra* note 273.

275. DMV has the discretionary authority to revoke a defendant's driver's license for up to six months under G.S. 20-16(a)(8) for a conviction of illegal transportation of alcoholic beverages.

Statute	Description of Offense	Punishment
18B-403.1(b), (e), -102(b)	Violation by seller of permit requirements for purchase of keg of malt beverage:	
	First violation	Warning
	Subsequent violation	Class 1 misdemeanor
18B-406, -102(b)	Transportation of unauthorized amount of alcoholic beverage	Class 1 misdemeanor[276]
18B-702(w)	Embezzlement by employee of local ABC Board	Class H felony
18B-903A	Making a false statement in application for reissuance of certain permits	Class 1 misdemeanor[277]
18B-1004, -102(b)	Selling or consuming alcoholic beverage after hours on licensed premises	Class 1 misdemeanor
18B-1005, -102(b)	Allowing violation of Chapter 18B, fighting, disorderly conduct, controlled substances violation, gambling, prostitution, or other unlawful act on licensed premises	Class 1 misdemeanor
18B-1005.1, -102(b)	Allowing sexually explicit conduct on licensed premises	Class 1 misdemeanor

Chapter 18C: North Carolina State Lottery

18C-131(d)	Lotteries:	
	Selling lottery ticket to person under 18	Class 1 misdemeanor
	Purchasing of lottery ticket by person under 18	Class 1 misdemeanor

Chapter 19: Offenses against Public Morals

Article 1: Abatement of Nuisances

19-4	Violation of abatement-of-nuisance injunction	Three to six months' imprisonment, $200 to $1,000 fine, or both

Chapter 19A: Protection of Animals

Article 3: Animal Welfare Act

19A-33	Operating pet shop, kennel, or auction without license	Class 3 misdemeanor, but limited to $5 to $25 fine[278]
19A-34	Acting as dealer without license	Class 2 misdemeanor[279]

276. *See supra* note 275.
277. This offense was enacted by S.L. 2018-100, effective for offenses committed on or after December 1, 2018.
278. Each day's operation without a license is a separate offense.
279. Upon conviction, animals in possession of the unlicensed dealer are subject to sale or euthanasia in the discretion of the Director of the Animal Welfare Section of the Department of Agriculture and Consumer Services.

Statute	Description of Offense	Punishment
19A-35	Failing to adequately care for animals	Class 3 misdemeanor and fine of not less than $5 per animal up to total of $1,000[280]
19A-36	Violation of Article 3 by dog warden	Class 3 misdemeanor and $50 to $100 fine[281]

Article 4: Animal Cruelty Investigators

19A-48	Interfering with animal cruelty investigator	Class 1 misdemeanor

Chapter 20: Motor Vehicles

Driver's License Violations

Driving without License or Violating Restrictions

20-7(a), -35	Operating motor vehicle without North Carolina license	Class 3 misdemeanor
20-7(a), -35	Driving class of motor vehicle that driver's license does not entitle person to drive	Class 3 misdemeanor[282]
20-7(a), -35	Failure to carry license while operating motor vehicle	Infraction
20-7(a1), -35	Operating motorcycle without having proper driver's license endorsement	Class 2 misdemeanor
20-7(e), -35	Operating motor vehicle in violation of driver's license restriction	Class 3 misdemeanor
20-7(f), -35	Operating motor vehicle with expired driver's license	Infraction
20-7(l), (m), -35	Operating motor vehicle in violation of restriction on instruction or learner's permit	Class 2 misdemeanor
20-7.1, -35	Failure to notify DMV of change of address on driver's license	Infraction

280. *See supra* note 279.

281. Each animal handled in a violation of the article is a separate offense.

282. It can be argued that Section 4 of S.L. 2013-385 did not specifically reduce this violation from a Class 2 misdemeanor to a Class 3 misdemeanor by stating in amended G.S. 20-35(a1) that it is a Class 3 misdemeanor when there is a "[f]ailure to obtain a license before driving a motor vehicle, in violation of G.S. 20-7(a)," because a person who commits this offense had a license but just not for the vehicle driven. Thus, this offense could be considered to fall within the catchall category in G.S. 20-35(a) (providing that a violation of Article 2 of Chapter 20 is a Class 2 misdemeanor unless a statute provides for different punishment). On the other hand, it can be argued that the language in S.L. 2013-385 could reasonably be interpreted to include failure to obtain a license for the motor vehicle driven. Given the ambiguity, this publication takes the position that the lesser punishment applies to a defendant who is charged with this violation. Thus, for offenses committed on or after December 1, 2013, this violation is a Class 3 misdemeanor. For an offense committed before that date, it is a Class 2 misdemeanor.

Statute	Description of Offense	Punishment
Age Limits		
20-10, -35	Operating public passenger vehicle if under age 18	Class 2 misdemeanor
20-10, -35	Person age 14 or under operating any road machine, tractor, etc., on highway	Class 2 misdemeanor
20-10.1, -35	Person under age 16 driving moped on highway or public vehicular area	Class 2 misdemeanor
20-11(c) through (l), -35	Holder of limited learner's permit, temporary permit, or limited provisional license driving motor vehicle in violation of restrictions applicable to permit or license	Class 3 misdemeanor[283]
Impaired Driving Instructor		
20-12.1	Instructing driver while impaired[284]	Class 2 misdemeanor
Driving with Suspended or Revoked License[285]		
20-16.1(b)(4), -28(a)	Violating limited driving privilege for excessive speeding	Class 3 misdemeanor[286]
20-21	Operating motor vehicle with license issued by another jurisdiction when driver's license or privilege to drive in North Carolina is suspended or revoked	See punishment under 20-28(a), below
20-28(a)	Driving while license is suspended or revoked when license was originally revoked for any reason other than impaired driving	Class 3 misdemeanor
20-28(a1)	Driving while license is suspended or revoked when license was originally revoked for impaired driving[287]	Class 1 misdemeanor
20-28(a1), -7, -35	Driving vehicle by restoree of suspended or revoked license without requisite financial responsibility	Class 3 misdemeanor[288]

283. G.S. 20-11(l) provides that failure to comply with a restriction concerning the time of driving or the presence of a supervising driver in the vehicle constitutes operating a motor vehicle without a license, which is also a Class 3 misdemeanor. Failing to comply with the restriction concerning the use of a mobile telephone while operating a motor vehicle is an infraction punishable by a fine of $25. Failing to comply with any other restriction, including seating and passenger limitations, is an infraction punishable by a penalty as provided in G.S. 20-176, which is not more than $100.

284. G.S. 20-16(8a) authorizes DMV to suspend the defendant's driver's license for a period of up to one year under G.S. 20-19(c). This offense is an implied consent offense under G.S. 20-16.2.

285. On receiving notice of a conviction of a moving offense when a person's driver's license was suspended or revoked, except a conviction under G.S. 20-28(a1) (driving without reclaiming license), DMV must revoke a person's driving license for an additional period: one year for a first revocation, two years for a second revocation, and permanently for a third or subsequent revocation.

286. Under G.S. 20-16.1(b)(4), the punishment for this offense is the same as for driving while license suspended under G.S. 20-28(a). The defendant must surrender his or her driver's license to the court as required by G.S. 20-24(a).

287. For a first offense under this subsection, the license is revoked for an additional year; for a second offense, two additional years; for a third or subsequent offense, permanently. The defendant must surrender his or her driver's license to the court. The licensee is entitled to apply for early restoration of the license according to the schedule set forth in G.S. 20-28(c).

288. The punishment for this offense is the same as for driving without a license (G.S. 20-7), which is punishable under G.S. 20-35.

Statute	Description of Offense	Punishment
20-28(a2), -7, -35	Driving without reclaiming revoked driver's license[289]	Class 3 misdemeanor[290]
20-28(a3), -7, -35	Driving after notification or failure to appear	Class 1 misdemeanor[291]
20-28(d), (a)	Driving motor vehicle while person is disqualified and driver's license is revoked:[292]	
	License originally revoked for impaired driving	Class 1 misdemeanor
	License originally revoked for any other reason	Class 3 misdemeanor
20-28(d)	Driving commercial motor vehicle during disqualification period	Class 1 misdemeanor[293]
Illegal Activity Relating to License		
20-29	Refusing to give uniformed officer information required by statute, such as name, address, or vehicle owner; or giving false information; or refusing to surrender or produce license upon demand of court or DMV	Class 2 misdemeanor
20-29	Motor vehicle driver involved in accident refusing to give information required by statute	Class 2 misdemeanor
20-29.1, -7(a), -35	Failing to observe restrictions imposed by DMV about kinds of motor vehicles licensee may operate	Class 3 misdemeanor
20-30(1), -35	Displaying or possessing any license or learner's permit known to be invalid	Class 2 misdemeanor[294]
20-30(2), -35	Counterfeiting, selling, lending, or knowingly permitting use of driver's license or learner's permit by one not entitled to do so	Class 2 misdemeanor[295]
20-30(3), -35	Displaying or representing as one's own a license not issued to person displaying it	Class 2 misdemeanor[296]
20-30(4)	Refusing to surrender to DMV a driver's license that has been revoked or suspended	Class 2 misdemeanor

289. This subsection involves reclaiming a driver's license after an immediate civil revocation for impaired driving under G.S. 20-16.5 and revocations for child support matters under G.S. 50-13.12 and 110-142.2.

290. *See supra* note 288.

291. After a conviction the person's driver's license must be revoked for an additional period of one year for the first offense, two years for the second offense, and permanently for a third or subsequent offense. The defendant must surrender his or her driver's license to the court as required by G.S. 20-24(a). G.S. 20-28(a3) also provides that the restoree of a revoked driver's license who operates a motor vehicle on a highway without maintaining financial responsibility is punished as for driving without a license.

292. The statute states that this violation "is punishable as provided in the other subsections of this section," which presumably means under G.S. 20-28(a).

293. For disqualification periods upon conviction, see G.S. 20-28(d)(1) through (3). The defendant must surrender his or her commercial driver's license to the court as required by G.S. 20-24(a). A defendant's Class C driver's license is not surrendered.

294. Under G.S. 20-16(a)(6) and G.S. 20-19(c), DMV may suspend a person's license for not more than one year for conviction of this offense.

295. *See supra* note 294.

296. *See supra* note 294.

Statute	Description of Offense	Punishment
20-30(5)	Using or allowing another to use false name or address in license application or renewal	Class 1 misdemeanor[297]
20-30(5)	Making false statement, concealing material fact, or otherwise committing fraud in applying for license or permit	Class 1 misdemeanor[298]
20-30(6), -35	Reproducing or possessing reproduced copy of license or permit	Class 2 misdemeanor
20-30(7)	Offering simulated license for sale	Class I felony
20-30(8), -35	Possession of more than one commercial driver's license or possession of commercial driver's license and regular driver's license	Class 2 misdemeanor
20-30(9)	Use of false license or permit in commission of felony	Class I felony
20-31	Making false affidavit or knowingly swearing falsely to any matter required to be sworn to by statute	Class I felony[299]
20-32, -35	Causing or permitting unlicensed minor to drive on highway	Class 2 misdemeanor
20-34, -35	Allowing motor vehicle to be driven in violation of driver's license law	Class 3 misdemeanor
Parking Privileges for Handicapped Drivers		
20-37.6(c3), -176	Selling handicapped license plate or windshield placard	Class 2 misdemeanor
20-37.6(e)(1), (f)(1)	Parking in handicapped space without displaying handicapped license tag or windshield placard	Infraction[300]
20-37.6(e)(2), (f)(1)	Using or attempting to use handicapped license tag or windshield placard when not entitled to do so	Infraction[301]
20-37.6(e)(3), (f)(1)	Parking in front of handicapped ramp or curb cut	Infraction[302]
20-37.6(e)(4), (f)(2)	Use of signs not conforming to 20-37.6(d) by person responsible for designating parking spaces as handicapped	Infraction[303]

297. Under G.S. 20-17(a)(8) and -19(f), DMV must revoke a person's license for one year when convicted of this offense. The defendant must surrender his or her driver's license to the court as required by G.S. 20-24(a).

298. *See supra* note 297. Also, if a person falsely certifies to DMV under G.S. 20-9(i)(3) that he or she does not appear on the National Sex Offender Public Registry, that person violates G.S. 20-30 and DMV must immediately revoke the person's driver's license after determining that the person does appear in the registry. G.S. 20-9(i)(4).

299. Under G.S. 20-17(a)(5), G.S. 20-17(a)(8), and G.S. 20-19(f), DMV must revoke a defendant's license for one year upon conviction of this offense. The defendant must surrender his or her driver's license to the court as required by G.S. 20-24(a).

300. This infraction is punishable by a penalty of at least $100 but not more than $250.

301. *See supra* note 300.

302. *See supra* note 300.

303. *See supra* note 300.

Statute	Description of Offense	Punishment
Special I.D. Card		
20-37.7, -37.7(e)	Engaging in fraud or misrepresentation in applying for or using special identification card	Class 2 misdemeanor

Commercial Driver's Licenses

Statute	Description of Offense	Punishment
20-37.12(a), -37.21(a)	Driving commercial vehicle without valid commercial driver's license with applicable endorsements	Class 3 misdemeanor[304]
20-37.12(b), -37.21(a)	Driving commercial vehicle in violation of out-of-service order	Class 3 misdemeanor[305]
20-37.18(a), -37.21(b)	Possessing commercial driver's license and failing to notify DMV within 30 days of traffic conviction	Infraction[306]
20-37.18(b), -37.21(b)	Possessing commercial driver's license and failing to notify employer within 30 days of traffic conviction	Infraction[307]
20-37.18(c), -37.21(b)	Failure to notify employer on next business day that commercial driver's license has been suspended, revoked, or canceled or that privilege to drive commercial vehicle has been lost	Infraction[308]
20-37.19(a), -37.21(c)	Failure to require employee to notify employer that commercial driver's license has been suspended, revoked, or canceled or privilege lost	Infraction[309]
20-37.19(b)(1), -37.21(c)	Knowingly allowing, permitting, or authorizing driver to drive commercial vehicle while commercial license has been suspended, revoked, or canceled, etc.	Infraction[310]
20-37.19(b)(2), -37.21(c)	Knowingly allowing, permitting, or authorizing driver to drive commercial vehicle when driver has more than one driver's license	Infraction[311]
20-37.19(b)(3), -37.21(c)	Knowingly allowing, permitting, or authorizing driver to drive commercial vehicle when driver, commercial motor vehicle being operated, or motor carrier operation is subject to out-of-service order	Infraction[312]

304. A violation is punishable by a fine of not less than $250 for a first offense and not less than $500 for a second or subsequent offense.
305. *See supra* note 304.
306. A violation of this infraction is punishable by a penalty of not less than $200 and not more than $500.
307. *See supra* note 306.
308. *See supra* note 306.
309. A violation of this infraction is punishable by a penalty of not less than $500 and not more than $1,000.
310. *See supra* note 309.
311. *See supra* note 309.
312. *See supra* note 309.

Statute	Description of Offense	Punishment
Vehicle Registration		
20-50, -111(1)	Owning a vehicle (including a moped) that is not registered with DMV or that is not displaying current registration plates[313]	Class 3 misdemeanor
20-57(c), -176(a1)	Failure to sign, display, or carry registration card	Infraction
20-62.1	Violating requirements involving purchasing vehicles for scrap or parts only	Class I felony with a minimum fine of $1,000
20-63(a)	Willfully failing to surrender illegible registration	Class 2 misdemeanor
20-63(d), -176(a), (c)	Failing to place registration plate at proper place on motor vehicle	Class 2 misdemeanor
20-63(e)	Failing to clean registration plates after being requested to do so by an officer	Class 3 misdemeanor
20-63(f)	Willfully operating motor vehicle with registration plate that has been altered	Class 2 misdemeanor
20-63(g)	Willfully altering, disguising, or concealing numbers on registration plate	Class 2 misdemeanor
20-67, -176(a1)	Failure to notify DMV of address change for vehicle registration card within 60 days after change occurs	Infraction
20-71(a), -177	Altering certificate of title, registration card, or application for such with fraudulent intent	Class I felony
20-71(a), -177	Forging or counterfeiting certificate of title or registration card	Class I felony
20-71(a), -177	Knowingly using an altered, forged, or falsified certificate of title or registration card	Class I felony
20-71(b)	Possessing or reproducing blank North Carolina certificate of title or facsimile with fraudulent intent	Class I felony
Salvage Titles		
20-71.4(a), (d)	Failing to disclose damage to vehicle	Class 2 misdemeanor
Transfer of Title or Interest		
20-72(b), -176(a), (c)	Failing to deliver certificate of title	Class 2 misdemeanor

313. G.S. 20-53.4 provides that mopeds must be registered with the Division of Motor Vehicles. Failure to do so is a violation of G.S. 20-111(1), the registration statute.

Statute	Description of Offense	Punishment
20-72(b)	Delivering or accepting certificate of title assigned in blank	Class 2 misdemeanor
20-72(b)	Filing false sworn certification with DMV under 20-72(b)	Class H felony
20-73(a)	Failing to apply for certificate of title within required time	Class 2 misdemeanor[314]
20-74	Knowingly making false statement about date vehicle was sold or acquired	Class 3 misdemeanor
20-75, -176(a), (c)	Dealer failing to deliver certificate of title	Class 2 misdemeanor
20-77(d)	Failing to report vehicle as unclaimed to DMV	Class 3 misdemeanor
Dealer Plates		
20-79(e)(1)	Driving a vehicle with dealer license plates in violation of restrictions	Infraction
20-79.1, -176(a), (c)	Improper use of temporary registration plates or markers	Class 2 misdemeanor
20-79.2	Sale, rental, lease, or other provision of a transporter plate	Class I felony
Marking Business Vehicles		
20-101, -176(a), (c)	Failing to mark certain business vehicles	Class 2 misdemeanor
Car Theft and Related Offenses		
20-102.1	Knowingly making false report of vehicle theft to DMV or officer	Class 2 misdemeanor
20-106	Receiving or transferring stolen vehicle	Class H felony[315]
20-106.1	Failure to return rented vehicle with intent to defraud	Class I felony
20-107	Injuring or tampering with vehicle	Class 2 misdemeanor
20-108(a)	Knowingly possessing, selling, receiving, etc., motor vehicle that has had any identification or serial number altered or removed	Class 2 misdemeanor
20-109	Altering or changing engine or other numbers	Class I felony

314. DMV may also impose a $15 civil penalty.

315. Conveyances used to conceal, convey, or transport property in violation of G.S. 20-106 are subject to forfeiture under G.S. 14-86.1.

Statute	Description of Offense	Punishment
Violation of Registration Provisions		
20-111(1)	Operating vehicle that is not registered with DMV or that is not displaying current registration plate	Class 3 misdemeanor
20-111(2)	Knowingly displaying or possessing altered, expired, or revoked registration card or plate	Class 3 misdemeanor
20-111(3)	Giving, lending, or borrowing registration plate for use on another motor vehicle	Class 3 misdemeanor
20-111(4), -176(a), (c)	Failing to surrender to DMV, upon demand, title certificate, registration card, or plate that has been suspended or canceled	Class 2 misdemeanor
20-111(5)	Using false names or addresses or concealing or misrepresenting material facts in registration application	Class 1 misdemeanor
20-111(6)	Giving, lending, selling, or obtaining title certificate for any purpose other than registration, sale, etc., of vehicle for which issued	Class 2 misdemeanor
Perjury		
20-112	Knowingly making any false affidavit or swearing or affirming falsely	Class I felony
Failure to Obey Directions of Officers or Firefighters		
20-114.1(a), -176(a), (c)	Willfully failing or refusing to comply with lawful order of law enforcement officer concerning traffic control	Class 2 misdemeanor
20-114.1(b), -176(a), (c)	Willfully failing or refusing to comply with lawful order of firefighter or rescue squad related to traffic control	Class 2 misdemeanor
Truck Route Violation		
20-116(h)	Failing to use truck route	Class 2 misdemeanor
Flag or Light at End of Load		
20-117, -115, -176(a), (b)	Failing to display flag or light at end of load	Infraction
Weigh Station Violations		
20-118.1, -176(c)	Failing to enter weigh station or temporary inspection or weigh site	Class 2 misdmeanor

Statute	Description of Offense	Punishment
Equipment Violations		
Tires		
20-122.1, -115, -176(a), (b)	Driving with unsafe tires	Infraction
Steering Mechanism		
20-123.1, -115, -176(a), (b)	Failing to maintain steering mechanism in good working order	Infraction
Speedometer		
20-123.2, -141(o)	Operating vehicle without working speedometer	Infraction[316]
Brakes		
20-124(a), -115, -176(a), (b)	Absence of brakes sufficient to stop and control vehicle	Infraction
20-124(a), -115, -176(a), (b)	Failing to maintain brakes in conformity with regulations	Infraction
20-124(c), -115, -176(a), (b)	Failing to maintain originally equipped brakes, including failing to maintain two separate means of applying brakes	Infraction
20-124(d), -115, -176(a), (b)	Absence of at least one brake on motorcycle used on highway	Infraction
20-124(e), -115, -176(a), (b)	Absence on trucks of brakes sufficient to stop vehicle within required distances	Infraction
20-124(e1), -115, -176(a), (b)	Absence of brakes acting on all wheels on specified trucks or truck-tractors with trailers	Infraction
20-124(h)	Selling any unapproved brake fluid or lining	Class 2 misdemeanor
Horns and Warning Devices		
20-125(a), -115, -176(a), (b)	Driving vehicle without a horn audible up to 200 feet in normal conditions	Infraction
20-125(a), -115, -176(a), (b)	Using siren, compression, or spark plug whistle when not allowed	Infraction
20-125(a), -115, -176(a), (b)	Using horn for other than reasonable warning or making any unnecessary loud or harsh sound by horn or other warning device	Infraction
20-125.1, -176(a), (b)	Motor vehicle not equipped with directional signals	Infraction

316. The penalty for this infraction may not exceed $25. A violation is a lesser-included offense of G.S. 20-141, except when the charge is speeding in excess of 25 m.p.h. over the posted speed limit.

Statute	Description of Offense	Punishment
Mirrors		
20-126(a) , -115, -176(a), (b)	Driving motor vehicle on streets without rearview mirror that provides unobstructed view	Infraction
20-126(a) , -115, -176(a), (b)	Driving loaded motor vehicle that renders rearview mirror ineffective without using mirror that reflects rear view	Infraction
20-126(b) , -115, -176(a), (b)	Operating vehicle without outside mirror on driver's side	Infraction
20-126(c) , -115, -176(a), (b)	Operating motorcycle on streets without rearview mirror that provides unobstructed view of at least 200 feet	Infraction
Windshield Wipers and Tinted Windows		
20-127(a) , -115, -176(a), (b)	Operating vehicle without windshield wiper for cleaning snow, rain, moisture, etc., from front windshield	Infraction
20-127(b), (d)	Driving vehicle on highway or public vehicular area with window not meeting window tinting restrictions	Class 3 misdemeanor
20-127(c), (d)	Tinted vehicle windshield that does not meet window tinting restrictions in 20-127(b)	Class 3 misdemeanor
Mufflers		
20-128(a), -115, -176(a), (b)	Driving motor vehicle when muffler not in sufficiently good working order to prevent excessive noise or smoke	Infraction
20-128(b), -115, -176(a), (b)	Using muffler cut-out	Infraction
20-128(c), -115, -176(a), (b)	Operating motor vehicle without required emission control devices	Infraction
20-128.1(a), (d), -176(a), (b)	Operating gasoline-powered motor vehicle that emits visible air contaminants for longer than five consecutive seconds	Infraction
20-128.1(a), (d), -176(a), (b)	Operating diesel-powered motor vehicle that emits visible contaminants of specific shade or density for longer than five consecutive seconds	Infraction
Lights		
20-129(a)(1), -115, -176(a), (b)	Failing to have lights on from sunset to sunrise	Infraction
20-129(a)(2), -115, -176(a), (b)	Failing to have lights on when person cannot be seen clearly 400 feet ahead	Infraction
20-129(a)(4)	Failing to have lights on when windshield wipers are in use due to rain, fog, etc.	Infraction[317]

317. The penalty for this infraction is $5; court costs may not be assessed.

Statute	Description of Offense	Punishment
20-129(b), -115, -176(a), (b)	Absence on vehicle of at least two headlamps	Infraction
20-129(c), -115, -176(a), (b)	Absence on motorcycle of headlamp complying with statutory requirements	Infraction
20-129(c), -115, -176(a), (b)	Failing to keep motorcycle lamps lighted while motorcycle is in use on highway or public vehicular area	Infraction
20-129(d), -115, -176(a), (b)	Absence of required rear lamps	Infraction
20-129(e), -115, -176(a), (b)	Absence of rear reflex mirror when bicycle operated at night	Infraction[318]
20-129(e), -115, -176(a), (b)	Absence of lighted front lamp when bicycle operated at night	Infraction
20-129(e), -115, -176(a), (b)	Absence of lighted rear lamp or cyclist not wearing reflective vest when bicycle operated at night	Infraction[319]
20-129(f), -115, -176(a), (b)	Absence of required lights on other vehicles (farm tractors, etc.)	Infraction
20-129(g), -115, -176(a), (b)	Selling or operating motor vehicle without two stop lamps or motorcycle without one stop lamp	Infraction
20-129(h), -115, -176(a), (b)	Absence of white backup lamps in working condition	Infraction[320]
20-129.1(1), -115, -176(a), (b)	Absence of two reflectors and one stop light on rear of bus or truck	Infraction
20-129.1(2), -115, -176(a), (b)	Absence of additional specified lights and reflectors on certain trucks or buses	Infraction
20-129.1(3), -115, -176(a), (b)	Absence of two clearance lamps on front and one stop light at rear on truck tractor	Infraction
20-129.1(4), -115, -176(a), (b)	Absence of specified lights and reflectors on certain trailers or semi-trailers	Infraction
20-129.1(5), -115, -176(a), (b)	Absence of specified lights and reflectors on certain large pole trailers	Infraction
20-129.1(6), -115, -176(a), (b)	Absence of required reflectors and stop lights on certain smaller trailers	Infraction

318. S.L. 2016-90, effective for offenses committed on or after December 1, 2016, requires a rear reflex mirror; prior law required a rear reflex mirror *or* a rear lighted lamp.

319. S.L. 2016-90 added a provision that a bicyclist at night may wear a reflective vest as an alternative to having a lighted rear lamp on the bicycle.

320. This offense was enacted by S.L. 2017-211, effective for offenses committed on or after March 1, 2018.

Statute	Description of Offense	Punishment
20-129.1(7), (8), -115, -176(a), (b)	Failure on vehicle of front-clearance lamps to reflect amber color, or rear lamps and brake lights to reflect red color	Infraction
20-129.1(10), -115, -176(a), (b)	Absence of combination marker lamp mounted on bottom side rail at or near the center of each side of certain trailers showing amber color	Infraction
20-130.1(a), (e)	Installing or using a red light on vehicle	Class 1 misdemeanor
20-130.1(c), (e)	Installing or using a blue light on vehicle	Class 1 misdemeanor
20-130.3, -115, -176(a), (b)	Driving motor vehicle in forward motion while displaying white or clear lights on rear of vehicle	Infraction
20-131(a), -115, -176(a), (b)	Failing to dim headlights	Infraction
20-134, -115, -176(a), (b)	Failing at required times to display certain lights on the front and rear of vehicle parked or stopped on highway	Infraction
Seat Belts		
20-135.2A	Failure of driver or front seat passenger to wear seat belt	Infraction[321]
20-135.2A	Failure of rear seat occupant to wear seat belt	Infraction[322]
20-135.2B	Transporting children in open bed of pickup truck	Infraction[323]
Smoke Screens		
20-136	Driving, using, or possessing vehicle with smoke screen mechanism	Class I felony[324]
20-136.1	Driving while viewing television, computer, or video player	Infraction
Child Restraint Systems		
20-137.1	Transporting child less than 16 years of age without being secured in passenger restraint system or seat belt. Additional requirement for child less than age 5 and less than 40 pounds and for child under age 8 and less than 80 pounds	Infraction[325]
Unlawful Mobile Phone Use		
20-137.3	Using mobile phone by driver under 18	Infraction[326]

321. The penalty under G.S. 20-135.2A(e) for this infraction is $25.50 plus specified court costs set out in the statute.
322. The penalty under G.S. 20-135.2A(e) for this infraction is $10; court costs may not be assessed.
323. The penalty under G.S. 20-135.2B(c) for this infraction is not more than $25 even if more than one child less than 16 years old is riding in the bed; court costs may not be assessed.
324. A conviction of this offense results in a mandatory DMV driver's license revocation under G.S. 20-17(a)(a)(3). The defendant must surrender his or her driver's license to the court as required by G.S. 20-24(a).
325. This infraction is punishable by a penalty not to exceed $25.
326. The penalty for this infraction is set at $25; court costs may not be assessed.

Statute	Description of Offense	Punishment
20-137.4	Using mobile phone while operating school bus	Class 2 misdemeanor[327]
20-137.4A	Using mobile phone for text messaging or email while operating school bus	Class 2 misdemeanor[328]
20-137.4A	Using mobile phone for text messaging or email while operating vehicle other than school bus	Infraction[329]

Rules-of-the-Road Violations

Impaired Driving

20-138.1, -179(f3)	Impaired driving, Aggravated Level One Punishment	Minimum 12 months to maximum 36 months imprisonment and maximum $10,000 fine[330]
20-138.1, -179(g)	Impaired driving, Level One Punishment	Minimum 30 days to maximum 24 months imprisonment and maximum $4,000 fine[331]
20-138.1, -179(h)	Impaired driving, Level Two Punishment	Minimum 7 days to maximum 12 months imprisonment and maximum $2,000 fine[332]
20-138.1, -179(i)	Impaired driving, Level Three Punishment	Minimum 72 hours to maximum 6 months imprisonment and maximum $1,000 fine[333]

327. This offense is punishable by a fine of not less than $100.

328. This offense is punishable by a fine of not less than $100.

329. This violation is punishable by a penalty of $100 and court costs.

330. The term of imprisonment may be suspended only if a condition of special probation is imposed to require service of imprisonment of at least 120 days and a requirement that the defendant abstain from alcohol consumption for a minimum of 120 days, as verified by a continuous alcohol monitoring (CAM) device. For additional provisions, see G.S. 20-179(f3). The defendant must surrender his or her driver's license to the court as required by G.S. 20-24(a) because there is a mandatory DMV driver's license revocation under G.S. 20-17(a)(2).

331. The term of imprisonment may be suspended only if a condition of special probation is imposed to require service of imprisonment of at least 30 days, or at least 10 days if the defendant is also required to abstain from alcohol consumption for a minimum of 120 days, as verified by a CAM device. For additional provisions, see G.S. 20-179(g) and (h1). The defendant must surrender his or her driver's license to the court as required by G.S. 20-24(a) because there is a mandatory DMV driver's license revocation under G.S. 20-17(a)(2).

332. The term of imprisonment may be suspended only if a condition of special probation is imposed to require service of imprisonment of 7 days or to abstain from consuming alcohol, as verified by CAM, for at least 90 days. For additional provisions, see G.S. 20-179(h) and (h1). The defendant must surrender his or her driver's license to the court as required by G.S. 20-24(a) because there is a mandatory DMV driver's license revocation under G.S. 20-17(a)(2).

333. The term of imprisonment may be suspended, but it must include one of the conditions set out in G.S. 20-179(i)(1) through (4). For additional provisions, see G.S. 20-179(i). The defendant must surrender his or her driver's license to the court as required by G.S. 20-24(a) because there is a mandatory DMV driver's license revocation under G.S. 20-17(a)(2). A defendant may be eligible for a limited driving privilege under G.S. 20-179.3(b)(1).

Statute	Description of Offense	Punishment
20-138.1, -179(j)	Impaired driving, Level Four Punishment	Minimum 48 hours and maximum 120 days imprisonment and maximum $500 fine[334]
20-138.1, -179(k)	Impaired driving, Level Five Punishment	Minimum 24 hours and maximum 60 days imprisonment and maximum $200 fine[335]
20-138.1, -179(f1)	Impaired driving, aider and abettor[336]	See Level Five Punishment, above
20-138.2, -179	Impaired driving in commercial vehicle	Punishable as provided in 20-179 for impaired driving (see punishment levels, above)[337]
20-138.2A	Operating commercial vehicle after consuming alcohol	Class 3 misdemeanor[338]
20-138.2B	Driving school bus, school activity bus, child care vehicle, ambulance, etc., after consuming alcohol	Class 3 misdemeanor[339]
20-138.2C	Operating commercial vehicle while possessing alcoholic beverages	Infraction
20-138.3	Driving by person under age 21 after consuming alcohol or drugs	Class 2 misdemeanor[340]

334. *See supra* note 333.

335. *See supra* note 333.

336. G.S. 20-179(f1) provides that a person convicted of impaired driving as an aider and abettor is subject to Level Five Punishment. The judge need not make any findings of grossly aggravating, aggravating, or mitigating factors in such cases. The defendant must surrender his or her driver's license to the court as required by G.S. 20-24(a) because there is a mandatory DMV driver's license revocation under G.S. 20-17(a)(2).

337. G.S. 20-17(a)(2)b. requires DMV to revoke the driver's license of a person convicted of this offense if the driver's alcohol concentration level was .06 or higher. Thus, a defendant convicted of this offense with an alcohol concentration that meets or exceeds this threshold must surrender his or her regular driver's license to the court as required by G.S. 20-24(a). G.S. 20-17.4 requires DMV to disqualify a person convicted of this offense from driving a commercial motor vehicle, and the defendant must surrender his or her commercial driver's license to the court as required by G.S. 20-24(a). For additional information concerning the effects of disqualification, see G.S. 20-17.5.

338. G.S. 20-138.2A(c) provides that notwithstanding G.S. 15A-1340.23, the Class 3 misdemeanor is punishable by a penalty of $100. A conviction of a first offense disqualifies the defendant from driving a commercial motor vehicle for 10 days, and the defendant must surrender his or her commercial driver's license and any Class A or Class B driver's license to the court as required by G.S. 20-24(a). A second or subsequent violation is punishable under G.S. 20-179 (see levels one through five set out for impaired driving in the chart above) and results in a mandatory DMV regular driver's license revocation under G.S. 20-17(a)(13) and disqualification of a commercial driver's license under G.S. 20-17.4(a)(6)—under these circumstances, the defendant must surrender these licenses to the court as required by G.S. 20-24(a).

339. G.S. 20-138.2B(c) provides that notwithstanding G.S. 15A-1340.23, the Class 3 misdemeanor is punishable by a penalty of $100. A second or subsequent violation is punishable under G.S. 20-179 (see levels one through five set out for impaired driving in the chart above) and results in a mandatory DMV regular driver's license revocation under G.S. 20-17(a)(14). G.S. 20-17(a)(14) requires DMV to revoke the driver's license of a person convicted of this offense, and the defendant must surrender his or her driver's license to the court as required by G.S. 20-24(a).

340. G.S. 20-13.2 requires a revocation of the defendant's driver's license for a conviction of this offense. The defendant must surrender his or her driver's license to the court as required by G.S. 20-24(a).

Statute	Description of Offense	Punishment
20-138.5	Habitual impaired driving	Class F felony[341]
20-138.7(a)	Transporting open container of alcoholic beverage after consuming alcohol	Class 3 misdemeanor[342]
20-138.7(a1)	Possession of alcoholic beverage in other than unopened original container, or consumption of alcoholic beverage, in motor vehicle's passenger area while on highway	Infraction
Reckless Driving[343]		
20-140(a), (d)	Driving carelessly and heedlessly	Class 2 misdemeanor[344]
20-140(b), (d)	Driving without due caution	Class 2 misdemeanor[345]
20-140(f)	Reckless driving of commercial motor vehicle	Class 2 misdemeanor[346]
Overloaded or Overcrowded Vehicle		
20-140.2, -176(a), (b)	Overloaded or overcrowded vehicle	Infraction
Using Controlled-Access Highways[347]		
20-140.3(1), -176(a), (b)	Driving across curb, dividing section, or dividing line	Infraction
20-140.3(2), -176(a), (b)	Making left, semicircular, or U-turn	Infraction
20-140.3(3), -176(a), (b)	Driving in wrong lane or wrong direction	Infraction

---

341. The defendant must be sentenced to a minimum active sentence of not less than 12 months, which may not be suspended, and it must run consecutively with and begin at the expiration of any sentence being served. The defendant's driver's license must be permanently revoked, and the defendant must surrender his or her driver's license to the court as required by G.S. 20-24(a).

342. A second or subsequent offense is a Class 2 misdemeanor, and G.S. 20-17(a)(12) requires a revocation of a defendant's driver's license. The defendant must surrender his or her driver's license to the court as required by G.S. 20-24(a).

343. Reckless driving convictions are subject to three provisions concerning the revocation or suspension of a driver's license:

1. A discretionary DMV suspension under G.S. 20-16(a)(9) and -19(a) is not to exceed six months for convictions within a 12-month period of one or more charges of reckless driving or aggressive driving and one or more charges of speeding in excess of 55 m.p.h. and not more than 80 m.p.h.
2. A mandatory DMV revocation for one year under G.S. 20-17(a)(6) and -19(f) for convictions within 12 months of (1) two charges of reckless driving, (2) two charges of aggressive driving, or (3) one or more charges of reckless driving and one or more charges of aggressive driving.
3. A mandatory DMV revocation for one year under G.S. 20-17(a)(7) and -19(f) for convictions of one charge of reckless or aggressive driving while illegally transporting intoxicants for the purpose of sale.

For the mandatory revocations, the defendant must surrender his or her driver's license to the court as required by G.S. 20-24(a).

344. *See supra* note 343.

345. *See supra* note 343.

346. *See supra* note 343.

347. G.S. 136-89.58 also creates certain controlled-access road offenses that roughly parallel those in G.S. 20-140.3, but the offenses in G.S. 136-89.58 are Class 2 misdemeanors.

Statute	Description of Offense	Punishment
20-140.3(4), -176(a), (b)	Driving onto or from any controlled-access highway when no established entrance and exit	Infraction
20-140.3(5), -176(a), (b)	Stopping, parking, or leaving vehicle on any part of right-of-way	Infraction
20-140.3(6), -176(a), (b)	Failing to yield right-of-way to vehicle when entering highway	Infraction
Motorcycles and Mopeds		
20-140.4(a)(1), (c)	Operating motorcycle or moped with more people than it is designated to carry	Infraction[348]
20-140.4(a)(2), (c)	Operating motorcycle or moped without approved safety helmet	Infraction[349]
Speeding[350]		
20-141(a), -176(a), (b)	Driving faster than is reasonable and prudent under conditions	Infraction
20-141(b), -176(a), (b)	Operating vehicle in excess of following speeds (with exceptions): 35 m.p.h. inside municipal limits and 55 m.p.h. outside municipal limits	Infraction
20-141(e), -176(a), (b)	Violating speed limit set by local authority for streets not in state highway system	Infraction
20-141(e1)	Violating speed limit on school property set and posted by local authority	Infraction with mandatory $250 penalty
20-141(f), -176(a), (b)	Violating speed limit set by local authority on streets in the state system and within corporate limits	Infraction

348. The violation is punishable by a penalty of $25.50 and specified court costs.
349. *See supra* note 348.
350. All speeding violations are subject to the following provisions concerning the suspension or revocation of a license:

1. A discretionary DMV suspension under G.S. 20-16(a)(10) and -19(b) not to exceed 12 months for a conviction of operating a motor vehicle over 75 m.p.h. when the maximum speed is less than 70 m.p.h.
2. A discretionary DMV suspension under G.S. 20-16(a)(9) and -19(a) not to exceed six months if a conviction within a 12-month period of (1) two or more charges of speeding over 55 m.p.h. and not more than 80 m.p.h., (2) one or more charges of reckless driving and one or more charges of speeding in excess of 55 m.p.h. and not more than 80 m.p.h., or (3) one or more charges of aggressive driving and one or more charges of speeding in excess of 55 m.p.h. and not more than 80 m.p.h.
3. A mandatory DMV suspension under G.S. 20-16.1 for 30 days upon conviction of exceeding the speed limit by more than 15 m.p.h. if the person was also exceeding 55 m.p.h. (including in work zone) at the time of the offense (or for 60 days upon conviction of a second or subsequent offense that occurred within one year of the first or prior offense).

The same provisions apply if the driver was exceeding 80 m.p.h.; see G.S. 20-16(a)(10a). For the mandatory revocations, the defendant must surrender his or her driver's license to the court as required by G.S. 20-24(a). A judge may grant limited driving privileges to a first offender under G.S. 20-16.1(a).

G.S. 20-141(o) makes G.S. 20-123.2 (defective speedometer) a lesser-included offense of a G.S. 20-141 violation, except if the charge is speeding in excess of 25 m.p.h. or more over the posted speed limit. G.S. 20-141(p) provides that a driver charged with speeding more than 25 m.p.h. over the posted speed limit is ineligible for a prayer for judgment continued (PJC).

Statute	Description of Offense	Punishment
20-141(g), -176(a), (b)	Violating minimum speed limit established on state highways or by local authorities	Infraction
20-141(h), -176(a), (b)	Operating vehicle at such slow speed as to impede normal and reasonable movement of traffic	Infraction
20-141(j1)	Driving more than 15 m.p.h. more than speed limit	Class 3 misdemeanor[351]
20-141(j1)	Driving more than 80 m.p.h.	Class 3 misdemeanor[352]
20-141(j2)	Driving in highway work zone in excess of posted speed limit	Infraction[353]
20-141(j3)	Driving commercial motor vehicle carrying load and violating speed restrictions	Class 2 misdemeanor
20-141(m), -176(a), (b)	Failing to reduce speed as necessary to avoid accident	Infraction
School Zones		
20-141.1	Violating speed limits set by the Board of Transportation or local authority for areas near schools	Infraction with mandatory $250 penalty
Racing		
20-141.3(a)	Engaging in prearranged speed competition with another motor vehicle	Class 1 misdemeanor[354]
20-141.3(b)	Willfully engaging in speed competition with another motor vehicle (not prearranged)	Class 2 misdemeanor[355]
20-141.3(c)	Allowing or authorizing others to use one's motor vehicle in prearranged speed competition	Class 1 misdemeanor[356]
20-141.3(c)	Placing or receiving bet or wager on prearranged speed competition	Class 1 misdemeanor[357]
Felony and Misdemeanor Death by Vehicle and Felony Serious Injury by Vehicle		
20-141.4(a1), (b)	Felony death by vehicle	Class D felony[358]

351. The defendant must surrender his or her driver's license to the court as required by G.S. 20-24(a) if the speed was more than 55 m.p.h. because this violation is subject to a mandatory DMV license revocation under G.S. 20-16.1, though a limited driving privilege may be granted.

352. The defendant must surrender his or her driver's license to the court as required by G.S. 20-24(a) because this violation is subject to a mandatory DMV license revocation under G.S. 20-16.1, though a limited driving privilege may be granted.

353. The penalty for a violation of this statute is $250 in addition to the penalty required for the speeding violation.

354. A conviction of this offense results in a mandatory DMV driver's license revocation under G.S. 20-141.3(d), and the defendant must surrender his or her driver's license to the court as required by G.S. 20-24(a).

355. There is a discretionary DMV driver's license revocation for a conviction of this offense under G.S. 20-141.3(e).

356. A conviction of this offense results in a mandatory DMV driver's license revocation under G.S. 20-141.3(d), and the defendant must surrender his or her driver's license to the court as required by G.S. 20-24(a).

357. *See supra* note 356.

358. G.S. 20-141.4(b)(2) provides that notwithstanding G.S. 15A-1340.17, an intermediate punishment is authorized for a defendant in Prior Record Level I. A conviction of this offense results in a permanent DMV driver's license revocation under G.S. 20-17(a)(9), and the defendant must surrender his or her driver's license to the court as required by G.S. 20-24(a).

Statute	Description of Offense	Punishment
20-141.4(a2), (b)	Misdemeanor death by vehicle	Class A1 misdemeanor
20-141.4(a3), (b)	Felony serious injury by vehicle	Class F felony[359]
20-141.4(a4), (b)	Aggravated felony serious injury by vehicle	Class E felony[360]
20-141.4(a5), (b)	Aggravated felony death by vehicle	Class D felony[361]
20-141.4(a6), (b)	Repeat felony death by vehicle	Class B2 felony[362]
Fleeing to Elude Arrest		
20-141.5(a)	Misdemeanor fleeing to elude arrest	Class 1 misdemeanor[363]
20-141.5(a), (b1)	Misdemeanor fleeing to elude arrest, proximately causing death	Class H felony[364]
20-141.5(b)	Felony fleeing to elude arrest	Class H felony[365]
20-141.5(b), (b1)	Felony speeding to elude arrest, proximately causing death	Class E felony[366]
20-141.6	Aggressive driving	Class 1 misdemeanor[367]
Failing to Stop for Railroad Signal or Tracks		
20-142.1(a), (d), -176(a), (b)	Failing to stop at railroad grade crossing	Infraction
20-142.1(b), (d), -176(a), (b)	Driving through crossing gate	Infraction
20-142.2, -176(a), (b)	Failing to stop at stop sign at dangerous railroad crossing	Infraction
20-142.3, -176(a), (b)	Certain vehicles failing to stop at railroad crossing	Infraction
20-142.4, -176(a), (b)	Operating or moving heavy equipment at railroad crossing without complying with statute	Infraction
20-142.5, -176(a), -176(b)	Driving into intersection, crosswalk, or railroad grade crossing and obstructing vehicles, pedestrians, or trains	Infraction

359. A conviction of this offense results in a permanent DMV driver's license revocation under G.S. 20-17(a)(9), and the defendant must surrender his or her driver's license to the court as required by G.S. 20-24(a).

360. *See supra* note 359.

361. G.S. 20-141.4(b)(1a) provides that notwithstanding G.S. 15A-1340.17, the court must sentence the defendant in the aggravated range of the appropriate Prior Record Level. A conviction of this offense results in a permanent DMV driver's license revocation under G.S. 20-17(a)(9), and the defendant must surrender his or her license to the court as required by G.S. 20-24(a).

362. A conviction of this offense results in a permanent DMV driver's license revocation under G.S. 20-179(a)(9), and the defendant must surrender his or her license to the court as required by G.S. 20-24(a).

363. A conviction of this offense results in a mandatory DMV driver's license revocation under G.S. 20-141.5(d), and the defendant must surrender his or her license to the court as required by G.S. 20-24(a).

364. *See supra* note 363.

365. *See supra* note 363.

366. *See supra* note 363.

367. For license revocation consequences for this offense, see *supra* note 343.

Statute	Description of Offense	Punishment
Speeding on Bridges		
20-144, -176(a), (b)	Speed limitation on bridges	Infraction
Lane Violations		
20-146(a), -176(a), (b)	Failing to drive on right half of highway	Infraction
20-146(a1)	Failing to operate self-propelled grain combine or other self-propelled equipment to right of centerline	Infraction
20-146(b), -176(a), (b)	Failing to drive in right lane when driving below speed limit	Infraction
20-146(c), -176(a), (b)	Driving to left of center on road with four or more lanes and two-way movement of traffic	Infraction
20-146(d)(1), -176(a), (b)	Failing to drive within a single lane or ascertain that lane change can be made safely	Infraction
20-146(d)(2), -176(a), (b)	Driving in center lane of road with three or more lanes and two-way traffic	Infraction
20-146(d)(3), -176(a), (b)	Failing to obey traffic control devices designating lanes	Infraction
20-146(d)(4), -176(a), (b)	Failing to obey devices prohibiting lane changes	Infraction
20-146(e), -176(a), (b)	Impeding traffic by using lane next to median of dual-lane highway at speed less than speed limit	Infraction
20-146.1(a), -176(a), (b)	Depriving a motorcycle of full use of a lane	Infraction
20-146.1(b), -176(a), (b)	Operating more than two motorcycles abreast in single lane	Infraction
20-146.2, -176(a), (b)	Violating HOV lane restrictions	Infraction
20-147, -176(a), (b)	Failing to drive vehicle on right half of highway in crossing intersection of two highways or of highway and railroad right-of-way	Infraction
20-147.1, -176(a), (b)	Operating passenger vehicle in left lane of multi-lane highway while towing another vehicle	Infraction
20-148, -176(a), (b)	Failing to pass vehicle going in the opposite direction to the right	Infraction

Statute	Description of Offense	Punishment
Improper Passing		
20-149(a), -176(a), (b)	Improper overtaking of vehicle when passing in same direction	Infraction
20-149(b), (b)(3)	Driver of overtaken vehicle failing to give way in favor of overtaking vehicle	Infraction
20-149(b), (b)(1)	Driver of overtaken vehicle failing to give way in favor of overtaking vehicle, collision resulting in serious bodily injury	Class 1 misdemeanor
20-149(b), (b)(2)	Driver of overtaken vehicle failing to give way in favor of overtaking vehicle, collision resulting in bodily injury or property damage	Class 2 misdemeanor
20-150(a), -176(a), (b)	Passing on left side of center of highway when movement cannot be made in safety	Infraction
20-150(b), -176(a), (b)	Improper passing on crest of grade or on a curve	Infraction
20-150(c), -176(a), (b)	Improper passing at railway grade crossing or at intersection	Infraction
20-150(d), -176(a), (b)	Driving to left side of centerline of highway on crest of grade or curve in highway	Infraction
20-150(e), -176(a), (b)	Passing vehicle when signs or markings clearly indicate that passing should not be attempted	Infraction
20-150.1, -176(a), (b)	Improper passing on the right	Infraction
Following Too Closely		
20-152(a), -176(a), (b)	Following vehicle more closely than reasonable and prudent	Infraction
20-152(b), -176(a), (b)	Failing to allow passing vehicle enough space to re-enter original lane of traffic	Infraction
Improper Turning		
20-153(a), -176(a), (b)	When approaching or turning right at intersection, failing to keep vehicle as close as practicable to right curb	Infraction
20-153(b), -176(a), (b)	When approaching intersection to turn left, failing to use extreme left-hand lane lawfully available	Infraction
20-153(b), -176(a), (b)	When turning left, failing to turn into a lane lawfully available to traffic leaving the intersection	Infraction
20-153(c), -176(a), (b)	Failing to obey lawful traffic control devices modifying general turning rules of 20-153	Infraction

Statute	Description of Offense	Punishment
20-154(a), -176(a), (b)	Starting, stopping, or turning without first seeing that movement can be made safely	Infraction
20-154(a), -176(a), (b)	Failing to sound horn before making movement that may affect pedestrians	Infraction
20-154(a), -176(a), (b)	Failing to give a signal when stopping, starting, or turning when another vehicle may be affected	Infraction
20-154(a), -176(a), (b)	Backing vehicle in unsafe manner or in manner that interferes with other traffic	Infraction
20-154(a1)	Violation of 20-154(a) that causes motorcycle or bicycle operator to change or leave travel lanes	Infraction with fine of not less than $200[368]
20-154(a1)	Violation of 20-154(a) that results in crash causing property damage or personal injury to motorcycle or bicycle operator or passenger	Infraction with fine of not less than $500[369]
20-154(a2)	Violation of 20-154(a) that results in crash causing property damage in excess of $5,000 or serious bodily injury to motorcycle or bicycle operator or passenger	Infraction with fine of not less than $750[370]
Failure to Yield Right-of-Way		
20-155(a), -176(a), (b)	Failure by driver on left to yield right-of-way when two vehicles enter intersection at about same time	Infraction
20-155(b), -176(a), (b)	Failing to yield to oncoming traffic when turning left	Infraction
20-155(c), -176(a), (b)	Failing to yield to pedestrian at crosswalk or regular pedestrian crossing	Infraction
20-155(d), -176(a), (b)	Failing to yield to vehicle already in traffic circle when approaching circle	Infraction
20-156(a), -176(a), (b)	Failing to yield to traffic when entering public highway from private road	Infraction
20-156(b), -176(a), (b)	Failing to yield right-of-way to law enforcement, fire, and other emergency vehicles with sirens and lights on	Infraction

368. S.L. 2016-90, effective for offenses committed on or after October 1, 2016, expanded the law to cover violations affecting bicycle operators.

369. *See supra* note 368.

370. The trial court has the authority to suspend the defendant's driver's license for up to 30 days but may allow a limited driving privilege. A violation is treated as a failure to yield right-of-way to a motorcycle for assessment of points under G.S. 20-16(c). S.L. 2016-90, effective for offenses committed on or after October 1, 2016, expanded the law to cover violations affecting bicycle operators.

Statute	Description of Offense	Punishment
Actions Prohibited in Emergencies		
20-157(a)	Upon approach of a fire, law enforcement, or rescue vehicle, etc., with lights and siren on, failing to stop on right side of road until emergency vehicle passes	Class 2 misdemeanor
20-157(b), (g)	Following closer than one block any fire apparatus traveling in response to fire alarm	Infraction punishable by $250 penalty
20-157(b), (g)	Driving into or parking within one block where fire apparatus has stopped to answer alarm	Infraction punishable by $250 penalty
20-157(c), (g)	Outside of city, following closer than 400 feet fire apparatus traveling in response to fire alarm	Infraction punishable by $250 penalty
20-157(c), (g)	Outside of city, driving into or parking within 400 feet where fire apparatus has stopped to answer alarm	Infraction punishable by $250 penalty
20-157(d), (g)	Driving over fire hose or any other equipment being used at fire	Infraction punishable by $250 penalty
20-157(d), (g)	Blocking firefighting apparatus from its source of supply	Infraction punishable by $250 penalty
20-157(e), (g)	Parking or leaving a vehicle within 100 feet of law enforcement, fire, or rescue vehicles that are investigating or assisting at accident	Infraction punishable by $250 penalty
20-157(f), (g)	Failing to change lanes or slow vehicle when passing stopped emergency vehicle	Infraction punishable by $250 penalty
20-157(h)	Failing to yield to emergency or public service vehicle and causing more than $500 in property damage	Class 1 misdemeanor
20-157(i)	Failing to yield to emergency or public service vehicle and causing serious injury or death in immediate area of emergency	Class I felony[371]
Funeral Processions		
20-157.1, -176(a), (b)	Violating funeral procession provisions by vehicles in procession or vehicles proceeding in same or opposite direction as procession	Infraction
Failing to Stop		
20-158(b)(1), -176(a), (b)	Failing to stop at intersection at stop sign or failing to yield right-of-way after stopping at stop sign	Infraction
20-158(b)(2), -176(a), (b)	Failing to stop at intersection or yield right-of-way when steady red light	Infraction[372]

371. DMV may suspend the defendant's driver's license for up to six months but may allow a limited driver's privilege.

372. Failing to yield the right-of-way to a pedestrian under G.S. 20-158(b)(2)b. is an infraction, and the court may assess a penalty under G.S. 20-158(b)(2)c. of not less than $100 and not more than $500.

Statute	Description of Offense	Punishment
20-158(b)(2a), -176(a), (b)	Failing at steady yellow light to proceed through intersection with due care	Infraction
20-158(b)(3), -176(a), (b)	Failing to stop at intersection and yield when flashing red light controls traffic in driver's lane	Infraction
20-158(b)(4), -176(a), (b)	Failing to proceed with caution and yield right-of-way when flashing yellow light controls intersection	Infraction
20-158(b)(5), -176(a), (b)	When required to stop at intersection, failing to stop at appropriate point specified in statute	Infraction
20-158(c)(1), -176(a), (b)	Failing to obey stop sign and yield right-of-way at place other than an intersection	Infraction
20-158(c)(2), -176(a), (b)	Failing to obey traffic light emitting steady red light at place other than an intersection	Infraction
20-158(c)(3), -176(a), (b)	Failing to stop and yield to pedestrians or other vehicles at flashing red light at place other than an intersection	Infraction
20-158(c)(4), -176(a), (b)	Failing to proceed with caution or yield at flashing yellow traffic light at place other than an intersection	Infraction
20-158(c)(5), -176(a), (b)	When required to stop at other than an intersection, failing to stop at appropriate point specified in statute	Infraction
20-158(c)(6)	Failing to stop when ramp meter is displaying circular red light	Infraction
Failure to Yield at Yield Signs		
20-158.1, -176(a), (b)	Failing to yield at yield sign at intersecting highway	Infraction
Driving through Safety Zones or on Sidewalks		
20-160, -176(a), (b)	Driving through or over safety zone or driving on sidewalk	Infraction
Failure to Yield Causing Serious Bodily Injury		
20-160.1	Failing to yield causing serious bodily injury	Infraction with mandatory $500 fine[373]
Parking on Highway		
20-161(a), -176(a), (b)	Parking or leaving vehicle on highway or bridge with speed limit less than 45 m.p.h., unless vehicle is disabled	Infraction
20-161(a1), -176(a), (b)	Parking or leaving vehicle on highway or bridge with speed limit 45 m.p.h. or greater, unless vehicle is disabled	Infraction

373. The statute mandates a driver's license or commercial driver's license suspension for 90 days, which requires the defendant to surrender his or her license to the court as required by G.S. 20-24(a).

Statute	Description of Offense	Punishment
20-161(b), -176(a), (b)	Parking or leaving vehicle on highway shoulder unless it can be clearly seen by driver from 200 feet	Infraction
20-161(c), -176(a), (b)	Failing to display warning devices for truck, truck tractor, etc., disabled on highway	Infraction
20-161.1, -176(a), (b)	Night parking on highway and vehicle's bright lights facing oncoming traffic	Infraction
20-162(a), -176(a), (b)	Parking vehicle on highway in front of private driveway, fire hydrant, fire station, etc.	Infraction
20-162(b), -176(a), (b)	Parking or leaving vehicle on highway or public vehicular area in area designated as fire lane	Infraction
20-163, -176(a), (b)	Leaving vehicle on highway or public vehicular area without stopping engine, setting brake, etc.	Infraction
Traveling Wrong Way on One-Way Street		
20-165.1, -176(a), (b)	Going wrong way on one-way highway under Department of Transportation jurisdiction	Infraction

Accident Responsibility Laws

Statute	Description of Offense	Punishment
20-166(a)	Failing to stop vehicle involved in crash resulting in serious bodily injury or death	Class F felony[374]
20-166(a1)	Failing to stop vehicle involved in crash resulting in injury	Class H felony[375]
20-166(b)	Driver involved in crash under 20-166(a) or (a1) failing to give name, address, driver's license number, etc.	Class 1 misdemeanor[376]
20-166(c)	Failing to stop vehicle involved in crash involving only property damage or injury or death if driver did not know of injury or death	Class 1 misdemeanor
20-166(c1)	Driver involved in crash under 20-166(c) failing to give name, address, driver's license number, etc.	Class 1 misdemeanor
20-166.1(a), (k), -176(c)	Failure by driver involved in reportable accident to notify appropriate law enforcement agency	Class 2 misdemeanor
20-166.1(b), (k), -176(c)	Failure by driver involved in reportable accident to furnish proof of financial responsibility to DMV on request	Class 2 misdemeanor

374. G.S. 20-17(a)(4) and G.S. 20-166(e) mandate a DMV driver's license suspension for this offense, the length of which is governed by both statutes. The defendant must surrender his or her driver's license to the court as required by G.S. 20-24(a).

375. G.S. 20-166(e) mandates a DMV driver's license suspension, the length of which is governed by the subsection, though the trial court may issue a limited driving privilege for a first conviction. The defendant must surrender his or her driver's license to the court as required by G.S. 20-24(a).

376. G.S. 20-17(a)(4) mandates a DMV driver's license suspension for this offense for a period of one year under G.S. 20-19(f). The defendant must surrender his or her driver's license to the court as required by G.S. 20-24(a).

Statute	Description of Offense	Punishment
20-166.1(c), (k), -176(c)	Failure by driver involved in collision with parked or unattended vehicle to report collision to owner and DMV	Class 2 misdemeanor
20-166.2(a)	Passenger leaving scene of accident or facilitating removal of vehicle in accident involving personal injury or death	Class H felony
20-166.2(a)	Passenger leaving scene of accident or facilitating removal of vehicle in accident involving property damage only or personal injury or death not known to driver	Class 1 misdemeanor
20-166.2(b)	Passenger's failure to transfer information to others involved in accident or to render assistance to injured	Class 1 misdemeanor

Transportation of Spent Nuclear Fuel

20-167.1	Transporting spent nuclear fuel without notifying State Highway Patrol	Class 3 misdemeanor punishable only by a minimum $500 fine

All-Terrain Vehicle Violations

20-171.15, -171.21	Parent or guardian permitting operation of all-terrain vehicle by child in violation of age restrictions	Infraction with maximum $200 penalty
20-171.17, -171.21	Selling all-terrain vehicle for unlawful use by underage person	Infraction with maximum $200 penalty
20-171.18, -171.21	Sale or operation of improperly equipped all-terrain vehicle	Infraction with maximum $200 penalty
20-171.19(a), -171.21	Operating all-terrain vehicle on highway or public vehicular area without eye protection or helmet	Infraction with maximum $200 penalty
20-171.19(a1), -171.21	Person under 18 years old operating all-terrain vehicle off highway or public vehicular area without eye protection or helmet	Infraction with maximum $200 penalty
20-171.19(b), -171.21	Authorization by owner of unlawful operation of all-terrain vehicle	Infraction with maximum $200 penalty
20-171.19(c), -171.21	Operating all-terrain vehicle while impaired by alcohol or drugs	Infraction with maximum $200 penalty
20-171.19(d), -171.21	Operating all-terrain vehicle in careless or reckless manner	Infraction with maximum $200 penalty
20-171.19(e), (f), -171.21	Operating all-terrain vehicle on highway (except when crossing the street) or an interstate highway	Infraction with maximum $200 penalty
20-171.19(g), -171.21	Operating all-terrain vehicle after dark without lighted headlight and taillight	Infraction with maximum $200 penalty
20-171.20, -171.21	Operating all-terrain vehicle without possessing safety certificate by person born on or after January 1, 1990	Infraction with maximum $200 penalty

Statute	Description of Offense	Punishment
Pedestrian Crosswalk Violations		
20-173(a), -176(a), (b)	Failing to yield to pedestrian at marked or unmarked crosswalk	Infraction
20-173(b), -176(a), (b)	Passing vehicle stopped at pedestrian crosswalk	Infraction
20-173(c), -176(a), (b)	Failing to yield to pedestrian or bicyclist when entering highway from private road or driveway	Infraction
20-174	Pedestrian unlawfully crossing roadway at other than crosswalk or along highway	Infraction
Standing, Sitting, or Lying in Street		
20-174.1	Sitting, standing, or lying on highway	Class 2 misdemeanor
Soliciting Rides, Employment, or Business on Highways		
20-175(a), -176(a), (b)	Standing in highway, except on shoulder, to solicit ride	Infraction
20-175(b), -176(a), (b)	Standing or loitering in highway to solicit employment, business, or contributions that impedes traffic	Infraction
Violating Limited Driving Privilege		
20-179.3(j), -28(a)	Violating restriction of limited driving privilege issued after conviction of impaired driving under 20-138.1	Class 1 misdemeanor[377]
20-179.3(j), -28(a)	Violating restriction of limited driving privilege issued after driver's license was forfeited under 15A-1331.1, revoked under 20-17.3, etc.	Class 3 misdemeanor[378]
Failing to Dim Headlights		
20-181	Failing to dim headlights	Infraction with maximum $10 penalty

377. For a first offense, the driver's license is revoked by DMV for an additional year; for a second offense, two additional years; for a third or subsequent offense, permanently. The defendant must surrender his or her driver's license to the court as required by G.S. 20-24(a).

378. For the length of a driver's license revocation, see *supra* note 377.

Statute	Description of Offense	Punishment
Equipment Inspection Laws		
20-183.8(a)(1)	Failure to have vehicle inspected as evidenced by lack of current electronic inspection authorization or otherwise	Infraction with maximum $50 penalty
20-183.8(a)(2)	Allowing electronic authorization to be issued to person's vehicle knowing vehicle was not inspected or was not inspected properly	Infraction with maximum $50 penalty
20-183.8(a)(3)	Issuing electronic authorization for vehicle knowing or having reasonable grounds to believe inspection was not performed or was performed improperly	Infraction with maximum $50 penalty
20-183.8(c)	Forging inspection sticker, buying or selling forged inspection sticker, etc.	Class I felony
Passing Stopped School Bus		
20-217(a), (e)	Passing stopped school bus	Class 1 misdemeanor with a minimum fine of $500[379]
20-217(a), (g)	Passing stopped school bus and striking person	Class I felony with a minimum fine of $1,250[380]
20-217(a), (g)	Passing stopped school bus and striking person, resulting in person's death	Class H felony with a minimum fine of $2,500[381]
Bus Driver Rules		
20-217(d)	Stopping school bus to receive or discharge passengers when passengers would have to cross roadway	Class 1 misdemeanor with minimum $500 fine
20-218(b)	Driving school bus with child passenger over 45 m.p.h. or driving school activity bus with child passenger over 55 m.p.h.	Class 3 misdemeanor
20-218.2	Driving nonprofit organization's activity bus for nonprofit purpose over 55 m.p.h.	Class 3 misdemeanor

379. This offense results in a one-year DMV driver's license revocation for a second conviction of a misdemeanor violation within three years, and requires a permanent DMV driver's license revocation for a third conviction of a misdemeanor within any time period. *See* G.S. 20-217(e), (g1). The mandatory revocations for a second or third conviction require a defendant to surrender his or her license to the court under G.S. 20-24(a). A person who commits this offense shall not receive a prayer for judgment continued (PJC) under any circumstances. G.S. 20-217(e).

380. A mandatory two-year DMV driver's license revocation is required for a conviction of this offense. For a second felony conviction, there is a permanent revocation. *See* G.S. 20-217(g), (g1). For any conviction, the defendant must surrender his or her driver's license to the court as required by G.S. 20-24(a).

381. A mandatory three-year DMV driver's license revocation is required for a conviction of this offense. For a second felony conviction, there is a permanent revocation. *See* G.S. 20-217(g), (g1). For any conviction, the defendant must surrender his or her driver's license to the court as required by G.S. 20-24(a).

Statute	Description of Offense	Punishment
Motor Vehicle Dealers		
20-287, -308	Engaging in motor vehicle business without license	Class 1 misdemeanor[382]
Insurance Violations		
20-313(a)	Operating or allowing vehicle registered in North Carolina to be operated without required financial responsibility[383]	Class 3 misdemeanor
20-313.1(a)	Making false certification concerning financial responsibility	Class 1 misdemeanor
20-313.1(b)	Giving false information to DMV concerning another's financial responsibility	Class 1 misdemeanor
Motor Carrier Safety		
20-384	Federal safety inspection violation	Infraction with maximum $50 penalty
20-396(a)	Seeking to evade regulations in Article 17 provided for motor carriers	Class 3 misdemeanor, but only punished by maximum $500 fine for first offense or maximum $2,000 fine for subsequent offense
20-396(b)	Motor carrier or person violating reporting obligations to DMV or Department of Public Safety	Class 3 misdemeanor, but only punished by maximum $5,000 fine

Chapter 44A: Statutory Liens and Charges

44A-12.1(c)	Filing, or attempting to file, false claim of lien on real property	Class I felony

Chapter 49: Children Born Out of Wedlock

49-2, -8	Nonsupport by parent of child born out of wedlock	Class 2 misdemeanor[384]

382. G.S. 20-287(b) and (c) also authorize DMV to levy and collect civil penalties.

383. S.L. 2015-125, effective for offenses committed on or after July 1, 2016, amended G.S. 20-309(a) to include a moped in the term "motor vehicle," and thus an owner who operates a moped must have financial responsibility.

384. G.S. 49-8 also authorizes the following dispositions: (1) suspension of sentence and continuance, (2) probation, conditioned on payment of support, (3) order to pay mother's medical expenses, and (4) order to sign recognizance for compliance with court order.

Statute	Description of Offense	Punishment

Chapter 50B: Domestic Violence

Statute	Description of Offense	Punishment
50B-3.1(i), (j)	While subject to protective order prohibiting possession or purchase of firearms:	
	Failing to surrender firearms, ammunition, permits to purchase firearms, or concealed firearm permits	Class H felony
	Failing to disclose information pertaining to firearms, ammunition, permits to purchase firearms, or concealed firearm permits	Class H felony
	Providing false information to court regarding firearms, ammunition, permits to purchase firearms, or concealed firearm permits	Class H felony
50B-4.1(a)	Knowingly violating valid protective order	Class A1 misdemeanor
50B-4.1(d)	Committing felony knowing that valid domestic violence protective order prohibits behavior	Felony one class higher than felony committed[385]
50B-4.1(f)	Knowingly violating valid domestic violence protective order after conviction of two offenses under Chapter 50B	Class H felony
50B-4.1(g)	Knowingly violating valid domestic violence protective order by failing to stay away from place or person while possessing deadly weapon	Class H felony
50B-4.1(g1)	Person subject to valid domestic violence protective order entering property operated as safe house or haven for domestic violence victims where protected person is residing	Class H felony
50B-4.2	Knowingly making false statement that domestic violence protective order remains in effect	Class 2 misdemeanor

Chapter 50D: Permanent Civil No-Contact Order against Sex Offenders

Statute	Description of Offense	Punishment
50D-10	Violation of permanent civil no-contact order against sex offender	Class A1 misdemeanor

Chapter 53: Banks

Statute	Description of Offense	Punishment
53-276, -287	Engaging in check-cashing business without license	Class I felony[386]

385. G.S. 50B-4.1(d) does not apply to convictions of Class A or B1 felonies or to convictions of the Class H felonies set out in G.S. 50B-4.1(f) or (g).

386. G.S. 53-287 provides that each transaction involving the unlawful cashing of a check, draft, or money order constitutes a separate offense.

Statute	Description of Offense	Punishment

Chapter 58: Insurance

Statute	Description of Offense	Punishment
58-2-161	False statement in support of or in opposition to claim for insurance benefits	Class H felony[387]
58-2-162	Embezzlement by insurance agent:	
	Of things valued less than $100,000	Class H felony
	Of things valued $100,000 or more	Class C felony
58-2-164(b)(1)	Rate evasion fraud	Class 3 misdemeanor[388]
58-2-164(b)(2)	Assisting, abetting, soliciting, or conspiring with another to engage in rate evasion fraud	Class 3 misdemeanor[389]
58-71-40, -71-185	Person acting as bondsman or runner without being licensed	Class 1 misdemeanor
58-71-95(5)	Failure by bail bondsman or runner to return collateral security of more than $1,500	Class I felony
58-71-95(6), -71-185	Bondsman or runner soliciting business in office of magistrate, courts, and other similar places	Class 1 misdemeanor

Chapter 62: Public Utilities

Statute	Description of Offense	Punishment
62-150	Entering conveyance by intoxicated person after being forbidden by driver	Class 1 misdemeanor
62-319	Riding on train unlawfully	Class 3 misdemeanor
62-322	Unauthorized manufacture or sale of switch-lock keys	Class 1 misdemeanor
62-328	Use of CB radio not authorized by Federal Communications Commission	Class 3 misdemeanor

Chapter 63: Aeronautics

Statute	Description of Offense	Punishment
63-26.1	Trespassing on airport property	Class 2 misdemeanor
63-27	Operating aircraft while impaired	Class 1 misdemeanor[390]
63-37.1	Obstructing takeoff or landing of aircraft at airport	Class 1 misdemeanor

387. G.S. 58-2-161(b) provides that conspiracy or solicitation to present a fraudulent statement is a Class H felony. The court may order as a condition of probation that the defendant pay restitution. In determining the amount of restitution, the reasonable costs and attorneys' fees incurred by the victim in investigating the claim may be considered part of the damage arising out of the offense.
388. In addition to any other penalties provided by law, the offense may be punishable by a fine up to $1,000.
389. In addition to any other penalties provided by law, the offense may be punishable by a fine up to $1,000.
390. A second or subsequent conviction of this offense is a Class I felony.

Statute	Description of Offense	Punishment
Chapter 66: Commerce and Business		
66-254.1	Sale by itinerant merchant of pseudoephedrine product and certain drugs:	
	First offense	Class 1 misdemeanor
	Second offense	Class A1 misdemeanor
	Third or subsequent offense	Class I felony
Chapter 67: Dogs		
67-4.2(a)(1), (c)	Leaving dangerous dog unrestrained on owner's property	Class 3 misdemeanor
67-4.2(a)(2), (c)	Permitting dangerous dog to go unrestrained beyond owner's property	Class 3 misdemeanor
67-4.3	Owning dangerous dog that attacks person and causes physical injury requiring medical treatment in excess of $100	Class 1 misdemeanor
67-12	Permitting dog to run at large at night	Class 3 misdemeanor[391]
Chapter 75A: Boating and Water Safety[392]		
75A-4, -18	Operating a vessel without identification number	Infraction
75A-6, -18	Operating a vessel without required equipment or lighting	Infraction
75A-10(b1)	Impaired boating	Class 2 misdemeanor with a minimum fine of $250
75A-10.3(a)	Death by impaired boating	Class D felony[393]
75A-10.3(b)	Serious injury by impaired boating	Class F felony[394]
75A-10.3(c)	Aggravated serious injury by impaired boating	Class E felony[395]
75A-10.3(d)	Aggravated death by impaired boating	Class D felony[396]

391. G.S. 67-12 provides that a person who violates this section shall be liable in damages to any person injured or suffering loss to property or chattels.

392. Under G.S. 75A-10.3(g), no person who has been placed in jeopardy upon a charge of death by impaired boating may be prosecuted for the offense of manslaughter arising out of the same death; and no person who has been placed in jeopardy upon a charge of manslaughter may be prosecuted for death by impaired boating arising out of the same death.

393. This offense was enacted by S.L. 2016-34 and is effective for offenses committed on or after December 1, 2016. Under G.S. 75A-10.3(f)(3), an intermediate punishment is authorized for defendants in Prior Record Level I, even though the sentencing grid would ordinarily call for an active sentence.

394. This offense was enacted by S.L. 2016-34, effective for offenses committed on or after December 1, 2016.

395. *See supra* note 394.

396. This offense was enacted by S.L. 2016-34, effective for offenses committed on or after December 1, 2016. Under G.S. 75A-10.3(f)(2), the court must sentence the defendant in the aggravated range of the appropriate Prior Record Level for this offense, regardless of whether aggravating factors are present.

Statute	Description of Offense	Punishment
75A-10.3(e)	Repeat death by impaired boating	Class B2 felony[397]
75A-13.3(c1), (c2)	Renting personal watercraft without liability insurance	Class 2 misdemeanor, but punishable only by a fine not to exceed $1,000

Chapter 84: Attorneys-at-Law

84-2	Engaging in practice of law by justice, judge, magistrate, full-time district attorney, full-time assistant district attorney, public defender, assistant public defender, clerk, deputy or assistant clerk, and certain others	Class 3 misdemeanor, but punishable only by a fine of at least $200
84-4, -8(a)	Unlawful practice of law	Class 1 misdemeanor

Chapter 90: Medicine and Allied Occupations

Article 5: North Carolina Controlled Substances Act[398]

90-95(a)(1), (b)(1)	Schedule I or II controlled substance:	
	Sale	Class G felony[399]
	Manufacture, delivery, or possession with intent to manufacture, sell, or deliver, except manufacture of methamphetamine	Class H felony

397. This offense was enacted by S.L. 2016-34, effective for offenses committed on or after December 1, 2016.

398. G.S. 90-96(a) and (a1) contain special conditional discharge provisions for sentencing first-time offenders found guilty of misdemeanor or felony possession of a controlled substance. A misdemeanor possession conviction may be expunged if the defendant was not over 21 years old when committing the offense and other requirements are met. *See* G.S. 15A-145.2(c), 90-96(e).

Several other statutory provisions apply to any violation of the Controlled Substances Act:

1. G.S. 90-95(e) provides for increased punishment for certain violations of the act. If the offense is a Class 1 misdemeanor and the defendant has previously been convicted under state or federal law of an offense punishable under Article 5, the defendant shall be punished as a Class I felon. Note that drug paraphernalia offenses are in Article 5B and thus do not qualify under this provision. If the offense is a Class 2 misdemeanor and the defendant has a prior conviction as set out above, the defendant is guilty of a Class 1 misdemeanor. A prior conviction that elevates an offense to a higher class may not be used to calculate a prior record or conviction level. If the offense requires a suspended sentence and the defendant has a prior conviction as set out above, he or she is guilty of a Class 2 misdemeanor.
2. G.S. 90-95(f) provides that a person convicted of an offense under Article 5 who is sentenced to an active term of imprisonment less than the maximum term that could have been imposed may also be sentenced to post-prison special probation to follow the active sentence for a period up to five years. Upon revocation of this special probation, the original term of imprisonment may be increased by no more than the difference between the active term of imprisonment served and the maximum active term that could have been imposed.
3. G.S. 90-95.3(a) authorizes the court to order a person convicted of a violation of Article 5 to make restitution to any law enforcement agency for reasonable expenditures made in buying controlled substances from the defendant. G.S. 7A-304(a)(7) and (a)(8) require the court to order a convicted defendant to pay $600 as a court cost in cases in which, as part of the investigation leading to the defendant's conviction, the North Carolina State Crime Laboratory or local government crime laboratory performed an analysis of any controlled substance possessed by the defendant or the defendant's agent.
4. Property used in connection with a violation of Article 5 is subject to forfeiture as provided in G.S. 90-112 and -112.1.

399. Sale and delivery of the same controlled substance is one offense, subject to one punishment. *See* State v. Moore, 327 N.C. 378 (1990).

Statute	Description of Offense	Punishment
90-95(a)(1), (b)(1a)	Manufacture of methamphetamine	Class C felony[400]
90-95(a)(1), (b)(2)	Schedule III–VI controlled substance:	
	Sale	Class H felony[401]
	Manufacture, delivery, or possession with intent to manufacture, sell, or deliver	Class I felony[402]
90-95(a)(2), (c)	Counterfeit controlled substance: creation, sale, delivery, or possession with intent to sell or deliver	Class I felony
90-95(a)(3), (d)(1)	Possession of Schedule I controlled substance	Class I felony[403]
90-95(a)(3), (d)(2)	Possession of Schedule II–IV controlled substance:	
	100 dosage units or less, except certain controlled substances	Class 1 misdemeanor
	Any quantity of cocaine, amphetamine, methamphetamine, or PCP, more than 4 dosage units of hydromorphone, or more than 100 dosage units of other substances	Class I felony[404]
90-95(a)(3), (d)(3)	Possession of Schedule V controlled substance	Class 2 misdemeanor
90-95(a)(3), (d)(4)	Possession of Schedule VI controlled substance:	
	Up to 1/2 oz. marijuana or 1/20 oz. hashish	Class 3 misdemeanor[406]
	More than 1/2 oz. marijuana or 1/20 oz. hashish	Class 1 misdemeanor
	More than 1 and 1/2 oz. marijuana or 3/20 oz. hashish, or any amount of synthetic tetrahydrocannabinols[405]	Class I felony
90-95(d1)(1)a.	Possession of precursor chemical with intent to manufacture controlled substance	Class H felony
90-95(d1)(1)b.	Possession or distribution of precursor chemical with knowledge or reasonable belief that it will be used to manufacture controlled substance	Class H felony
90-95(d1)(1)c.	Possession of pseudoephedrine product if person has prior conviction of possession or manufacture of methamphetamine	Class H felony

400. Packaging, repackaging, labeling, or relabeling methamphetamine are Class H felonies even though those actions might be considered forms of manufacturing.

401. *See supra* note 399.

402. G.S. 90-95(b)(2) provides that the transfer for no remuneration of less than 5 grams of marijuana does not constitute a delivery in violation of G.S. 90-95(a)(1). A former provision exempting transfers of less than 2.5 grams of a synthetic cannabinoid was repealed in 2017 by S.L. 2017-115.

403. If the controlled substance is MDPV and the quantity is 1 gram or less, the violation is a Class 1 misdemeanor.

404. In *State v. Jones*, 358 N.C. 473 (2004), the court held that possession of cocaine in violation of G.S. 90-95(a)(3) is a felony and therefore a conviction of that offense may serve as an underlying felony in a habitual felon prosecution.

405. Former provisions on synthetic cannabinoid quantities were removed in 2017 when synthetic cannabinoids were reclassified as a Schedule I controlled substance for offenses committed on or after December 1, 2017. S.L. 2017-115.

406. A sentence of imprisonment must be suspended, and the sentencing judge may not impose a period of imprisonment as a special condition of probation. *See* G.S. 90-95(d)(4).

Statute	Description of Offense	Punishment
90-95(d1)(2)a.	Possession of precursor chemical with intent to manufacture methamphetamine	Class F felony
90-95(d1)(2)b.	Possession or distribution of precursor chemical with knowledge or reasonable belief that it will be used to manufacture methamphetamine	Class F felony
90-95(e)(5), (a)(1)	Sale or delivery of controlled substance in violation of 90-95(a)(1):[407]	
	By person 18 or older to person under 16 but over 13 or to pregnant female	Class D felony
	By person 18 or older to person 13 or younger	Class C felony
90-95(e)(8), (a)(1)	Violation of 90-95(a)(1) by person 21 or older within 1,000 feet of elementary or secondary school or licensed child care center	Class E felony[408]
90-95(e)(9), (a)(3)	Possession of controlled substance in prison or jail	Class H felony
90-95(e)(10), (a)(1)	Violation of 90-95(a)(1) by person 21 or older on or within 1,000 feet of public park	Class E felony[409]
90-95(h)(1)	Trafficking in marijuana:[410]	
	More than 10 and less than 50 pounds	Class H drug-trafficking felony; fine of not less than $5,000
	50–1,999 pounds	Class G drug-trafficking felony; fine of not less than $25,000

407. G.S. 90-95(e)(5) does not specifically address the consequences of transferring less than 5 grams of marijuana for no remuneration. *Compare* G.S. 90-95(e)(8) (stating that such a transfer does not constitute a delivery in violation of G.S. 90-95(a)(1)). Because a sale or delivery in violation of G.S. 90-95(a)(1) is a required element of this offense, however, such a transfer may not constitute a violation of G.S. 90-95(e)(5). *See* G.S. 90-95(b)(2) (stating that such a transfer does not constitute a delivery in violation of G.S. 90-95(a)(1)).

408. The statute specifically provides that a transfer of less than 5 grams of marijuana for no remuneration is not a delivery for this offense.

409. *See supra* note 408.

410. A defendant convicted of drug trafficking is not sentenced according to the usual structured sentencing rules. A defendant convicted of drug trafficking must be fined as set forth in the text and the following minimum and maximum sentences apply regardless of the person's prior record level:

Class C drug-trafficking felony: Minimum 225 months; maximum 282 months.
Class D drug-trafficking felony: Minimum 175 months; maximum 222 months.
Class E drug-trafficking felony: Minimum 90 months; maximum 120 months.
Class F drug-trafficking felony: Minimum 70 months; maximum 93 months.
Class G drug-trafficking felony: Minimum 35 months; maximum 51months.
Class H drug-trafficking felony: Minimum 25 months; maximum 39 months.

G.S. 90-95(h)(5) provides that the court may reduce the fine, impose a prison term less than the applicable minimum, or suspend the prison term and place the person on probation upon a finding that the person provided "substantial assistance" in the prosecution of others. *See also* State v. Saunders, 131 N.C. 551 (1998) (in imposing sentence after finding substantial assistance, court is not required to impose minimum sentence prescribed under structured sentencing). G.S. 90-95(h)(6) provides that sentences imposed under G.S. 90-95(h) must run consecutively with, and begin at the expiration of, any other sentences being served by the defendant. When two or more offenses are being disposed of in the same proceeding, however, the court is not required to impose consecutive sentences. *See* State v. Thomas, 85 N.C. App. 319 (1987) (construing similar consecutive sentencing provisions).

Statute	Description of Offense	Punishment
	2,000–9,999 pounds	Class F drug-trafficking felony; fine of not less than $50,000
	10,000 pounds or more	Class D drug-trafficking felony; fine of not less than $200,000
90-95(h)(1a)	Trafficking in synthetic cannabinoids:[411]	
	More than 50 but less than 250 dosage units	Class H drug-trafficking felony; fine of not less than $5,000
	250–1,249 dosage units	Class G drug-trafficking felony; fine of not less than $25,000
	1,250–3,749 dosage units	Class F drug-trafficking felony; fine of not less than $50,000
	3,750 dosage units or more	Class D drug-trafficking felony; fine of not less than $200,000
90-95(h)(2)	Trafficking in methaqualone:[412]	
	1,000–4,999 dosage units	Class G drug-trafficking felony; fine of not less than $25,000
	5,000–9,999 dosage units	Class F drug-trafficking felony; fine of not less than $50,000
	10,000 dosage units or more	Class D drug-trafficking felony; fine of not less than $200,000
90-95(h)(3)	Trafficking in cocaine:[413]	
	28–199 grams	Class G drug-trafficking felony; fine of not less than $50,000
	200–399 grams	Class F drug-trafficking felony; fine of not less than $100,000
	400 grams or more	Class D drug-trafficking felony; fine of not less than $250,000
90-95(h)(3b)	Trafficking in methamphetamine:[414]	
	28–199 grams	Class F drug-trafficking felony; fine of not less than $50,000
	200–399 grams	Class E drug-trafficking felony; fine of not less than $100,000
	400 grams or more	Class C drug-trafficking felony; fine of not less than $250,000

411. *See supra* note 410.
412. *See supra* note 410.
413. *See supra* note 410.
414. *See supra* note 410.

Statute	Description of Offense	Punishment
90-95(h)(3c)	Trafficking in amphetamine:[415]	
	28–199 grams	Class H drug-trafficking felony; fine of not less than $5,000
	200–399 grams	Class G drug-trafficking felony; fine of not less than $25,000
	400 grams or more	Class E drug-trafficking felony; fine of not less than $100,000
90-95(h)(3d)	Trafficking in substituted cathinones:[416]	
	28–199 grams	Class F drug-trafficking felony; fine of not less than $50,000
	200–399 grams	Class E drug-trafficking felony; fine of not less than $100,000
	400 grams or more	Class C drug-trafficking felony; fine of not less than $250,000
90-95(h)(4)	Trafficking in opium, opiate, opioid, or heroin:[417]	
	4–13 grams	Class F drug-trafficking felony; fine of not less than $50,000
	14–27 grams	Class E drug-trafficking felony; fine of not less than $100,000
	28 grams or more	Class C drug-trafficking felony; fine of not less than $500,000
90-95(h)(4a)	Trafficking in LSD:[418]	
	100–499 dosage units	Class G drug-trafficking felony; fine of not less than $25,000
	500–999 dosage units	Class F drug-trafficking felony; fine of not less than $50,000
	1,000 dosage units or more	Class D drug-trafficking felony; fine of not less than $200,000
90-95(h)(4b)	Trafficking in MDA/MDMA:[419]	
	100–499 dosage units or 28–199 grams	Class G drug-trafficking felony; fine of not less than $25,000

415. *See supra* note 410.

416. *See supra* note 410. S.L. 2018-44, effective for offenses committed on or after December 1, 2018, replaced references to MDPV with the broader term substituted cathinones. The same act deleted former subdivision G.S. 90-95(h)(3e), trafficking in mephedrone, presumably on the understanding that mephedrone is a substituted cathinone covered under amended G.S. 90-95(h)(3d).

417. *See supra* note 410. S.L. 2018-44, effective for offenses committed on or after December 1, 2018, added opioids to the coverage of this subdivision. Before the addition, the law covered only opium, opiates, and heroin, which probably did not include opioids—defined by G.S. 90-87(18a) as any "synthetic narcotic drug having opiate-like activities but is not derived from opium."

418. *See supra* note 410.

419. *See supra* note 410.

Statute	Description of Offense	Punishment
	500–999 dosage units or 200–399 grams	Class F drug-trafficking felony; fine of not less than $50,000
	1,000 dosage units, or 400 grams, or more	Class D drug-trafficking felony; fine of not less than $250,000
90-95(i)	Conspiracy to commit drug-trafficking offense	Punishable by same penalties as for drug-trafficking felony defendant conspired to commit[420]
90-95.1	Continuing criminal enterprise	Class C felony; forfeiture of enterprise profits and other property set out in statute
90-95.4(a), -95(a)(1)	Hiring or intentionally using minor to violate 90-95(a)(1):	
	When defendant is at least 18 but less than 21 and minor is more than 13	Felony one class greater than violation for which minor was hired
	When defendant is at least 18 but less than 21 and minor is 13 or younger	Felony two classes greater than violation for which minor was hired
90-95.4(b), -95(a)(1)	Hiring or intentionally using minor to violate 90-95(a)(1):[421]	
	When defendant is 21 or older and minor is more than 13	Felony three classes greater than violation for which minor was hired
	When defendant is 21 or older and minor is 13 or younger	Felony four classes greater than violation for which minor was hired
90-95.6, -95(a)(1)	Promotion by person 21 or older of violation of 90-95(a)(1) by minor	Class D felony
90-95.7, -95(a)(1)	Purchasing or receiving controlled substance by person 21 or older from minor 13 or younger who violates 90-95(a)(1)	Class G felony

420. Under G.S. 90-95(i), a drug-trafficking conspiracy is the same class of offense as a completed drug-trafficking offense and is subject to the same mandatory minimum penalties and exceptions. *See supra* note 410. However, a drug-trafficking conspiracy is subject to a limitation not applicable to a completed trafficking offense. In *State v. Worthington*, 84 N.C. App. 150 (1987), the court held that a defendant may not be convicted of both a trafficking conspiracy to possess a controlled substance and a trafficking conspiracy to sell a controlled substance when the evidence shows only one agreement, even though the agreement involves more than one substantive offense. *Compare* State v. Perry, 316 N.C. 87 (1986) (approving separate charges and convictions for trafficking by possession, trafficking by manufacturing, and trafficking by transporting, even when the same contraband material is used in each offense).

421. A person 21 or older who hires, employs, or intentionally uses a person under 18 to commit a violation of G.S. 90-95 is liable in a civil action for drug addiction proximately caused by the violation. *See* G.S. 90-95.5.

Statute	Description of Offense	Punishment
90-98	Controlled Substances Act:	
	Conspiracy to violate	Same class as offense for which conspiracy created
	Attempt to violate	Same class as offense attempted[422]
90-108(a)(1)	Impersonating a licensed practitioner	Class 1 misdemeanor[423]
90-108(a)(2)	Unlawful distribution by registrant or practitioner	Class 1 misdemeanor[424]
90-108(a)(3), (a)(8), (a)(9)	Violating registration provisions relating to authorized manufacture or distribution	Class 1 misdemeanor[425]
90-108(a)(5)	Failing to keep or furnish records required by Article 5	Class 1 misdemeanor[426]
90-108(a)(7)	Maintaining building or vehicle for use by persons violating Article 5 or for keeping or selling controlled substance	Class 1 misdemeanor[427]
90-108(a)(7), (b)(1)	Violating 90-108(a)(7) while fortifying structure with intent to impede law enforcement entry	Class I felony
90-108(a)(10)	Obtaining controlled substance by fraud or deception	Class I felony[428]
90-108(a)(13)	Obtaining controlled substance by use of legal prescription obtained by misrepresentation	Class 1 misdemeanor[429]
90-108(a)(14), (b)(2)	Embezzlement of controlled substance by a registrant, a practitioner, or an employee of a registrant or practitioner	Class G felony[430]
90-108(a)(15), (b)(2)	Embezzlement of controlled substance by certain persons who are not registrants, practitioners, or their employees	Class G felony[431]

422. Under G.S. 90-98, an attempt to commit a drug-trafficking offense is the same class of offense as the completed offense, but it is subject to the regular structured sentencing grid; the mandatory minimum penalties for a completed drug-trafficking offense are not applicable to an attempt. *See* State v. Clark, 137 N.C. App. 90 (2000).

423. G.S. 90-108(b) provides that if the criminal pleading alleges that the violation was committed intentionally, and upon trial it is specifically found that the violation was committed intentionally, the violation shall be a Class I felony.

424. *See supra* note 423.

425. *See supra* note 423.

426. *See supra* note 423.

427. The court in *State v. Bright*, 78 N.C. App. 239 (1985), considered the applicability of G.S. 90-108(b) to this offense. *See supra* note 423. The court held that maintaining a vehicle with knowledge that it is used in connection with controlled substances is a misdemeanor, while maintaining a vehicle with intent that it be so used is a Class I felony.

428. The court in *State v. Church*, 73 N.C. App. 645 (1985), held that because a commission of this offense is by definition intentional and G.S. 90-108(b) provides that an intentional violation of G.S. 90-108 is a Class I felony, a misdemeanor offense under G.S. 90-108(a)(10) does not exist.

429. *See supra* note 423.

430. S.L. 2018-44, effective for offenses committed on or after December 1, 2018, added registrants and practitioners to this subdivision (previously it covered only employees of registrants and practitioners). For offenses committed on or after December 1, 2018, this offense is a Class E felony when committed by a person who intentionally diverts a controlled substance by means of dilution or substitution. G.S. 90-108(b)(3).

431. This offense was added by S.L. 2018-44, effective for offenses committed on or after December 1, 2018. This offense is a Class E felony when committed by a person who intentionally diverts a controlled substance by means of dilution or substitution. G.S. 90-108(b)(3).

Statute	Description of Offense	Punishment
Article 5A: North Carolina Toxic Vapors Act[432]		
90-113.10, -113.13	Inhaling fumes for purpose of intoxication	Class 1 misdemeanor
90-113.10A, -113.13	Manufacturing, selling, delivering, or possessing an alcohol vaporizing device	Class 1 misdemeanor
90-113.11, -113.13	Possession of substance for purpose of inhaling for intoxication	Class 1 misdemeanor
90-113.12, -113.13	Sale or delivery of, or possession with intent to sell or deliver, substance to induce intoxication, with knowledge of intended illegal use	Class 1 misdemeanor
Article 5B: Drug Paraphernalia		
90-113.22	Possession of paraphernalia other than marijuana paraphernalia	Class 1 misdemeanor
90-113.22A	Possession of marijuana paraphernalia	Class 3 misdemeanor
90-113.23	Delivery, possession with intent to deliver, or manufacture with intent to deliver	Class 1 misdemeanor
90-113.23(c)	Delivery by person over 18 to minor at least 3 years younger	Class I felony
90-113.24	Advertisement of paraphernalia	Class 2 misdemeanor
Article 5D: Control of Methamphetamine Precursors		
90-113.56(a)	Violation by retailer of restrictions concerning pseudoephedrine in 90-113.52 through -113.54:[433]	
	First offense	Class A1 misdemeanor
	Subsequent offense	Class I felony
90-113.56(b)	Violation by purchaser or employee of retailer of restrictions concerning pseudoephedrine in 90-113.52 through -113.54:	

432. G.S. 90-113.14(a) and (a1) contain special conditional discharge provisions for sentencing first-time offenders who violate G.S. 90-113.10 or -113.11.

433. A retailer convicted of a third offense on the premises of a single establishment is prohibited under G.S. 90-113.56(a) from selling pseudoephedrine products at that establishment. G.S. 90-113.56(c) provides that a retailer who fails to train employees in accordance with G.S. 90-113.55, supervise them in transactions involving pseudoephedrine products, or discipline them for violations is subject to a fine of up to $500 for a first violation, up to $750 for a second violation, and up to $1,000 for a third or subsequent violation. These sanctions, though labeled "fines," appear to be civil penalties, imposed administratively and not as part of a criminal case.

Statute	Description of Offense	Punishment
	First offense	Class 1 misdemeanor
	Second offense	Class A1 misdemeanor
	Third or subsequent offense	Class I felony

Article 5E: North Carolina Controlled Substances Reporting System Act

90-113.74(k)(1)	Accessing prescription information in the controlled substances reporting system for an unauthorized purpose by certain persons	Class I felony[434]
90-113.74(k)(2)	Disclosing or disseminating information in the controlled substances reporting system for an unauthorized purpose by certain persons	Class I felony[435]
90-113.74(k)(3)	Obtaining, disclosing, or disseminating prescription information for commercial advantage, personal gain, or to maliciously harm any person	Class H felony[436]

Article 5F: Control of Potential Drug Paraphernalia Products

90-113.82, -113.83(a)	Violation of restrictions on glass tubes or splitters in 90-113.82 by retailer or employee of retailer	Class 2 misdemeanor
90-113.82(b), -113.83(b)	False statement in fulfilling requirements in 90-113.82(b)	Class 1 misdemeanor

Chapter 95: Department of Labor and Labor Regulations

95-111.11(b), -111.13(i)	Operating amusement device, or knowingly permitting operator to operate device, while impaired:[437]	
	First offense resulting in death	Class 2 misdemeanor; fine up to $10,000
	Second offense resulting in death	Class 1 misdemeanor; fine up to $20,000
95-111.13(j)	Violating provision of Article 3B (amusement device safety), G.S. Chapter 95, causing serious injury or death	Class E felony, with a mandatory fine[438]

434. This offense was added by S.L. 2018-44, effective for offenses committed on or after December 1, 2018. Any person convicted of this offense is permanently barred from accessing the controlled substances reporting system.

435. *See supra* note 434.

436. *See supra* note 434.

437. These statutory provisions do not bar the prosecution for any appropriate degree of homicide. *See* G.S. 95-111.13(i). A person who violates G.S. 95-111.11(b) is also subject to a civil penalty of up to $1,000, imposed by the Commissioner of Labor. *See* G.S. 95-111.13(e).

438. A fine must be imposed in addition to any other punishment.

Statute	Description of Offense	Punishment
95-125.3(g)	Violating any provision of Article 15 (passenger tramway safety), G.S. Chapter 95, causing serious injury or death is a Class E felony, which shall include a fine	Class E felony[439]

Chapter 96: Employment Security

96-18(a)	False statement to obtain benefit:	
	Value of benefit wrongfully obtained is $400 or less	Class 1 misdemeanor
	Value of benefit wrongfully obtained is more than $400	Class I felony
96-18(b)	Violations by employer:	
	False statement to avoid or reduce benefit or contribution	Class 1 misdemeanor
	Failing to produce required records	Class 1 misdemeanor
96-18(c)	Other violations of employment security laws	Class 1 misdemeanor

Chapter 97: Workers' Compensation Act

97-88.2(a)	False statement to obtain or deny benefit:	
	If amount is less than $1,000	Class 1 misdemeanor
	If amount is $1,000 or more	Class H felony
97-88.2(c)	Threatening criminal prosecution to coerce employee to agree to or forego compensation	Class H felony

Chapter 105: Taxation

105-236(a)(7)	Attempting to evade or defeat tax	Class H felony
105-236(a)(8)	Failing to collect, withhold, or pay over tax	Class 1 misdemeanor
105-236(a)(9)	Failing to file return, supply information, or pay tax	Class 1 misdemeanor
105-236(a)(9a)	Aiding presentation of false return:	
	By income tax return preparer if tax fraudulently evaded in 1 year is $100,000 or more	Class C felony
	By income tax return preparer if tax fraudulently evaded in 1 year is less than $100,000	Class F felony
	By person who is not income tax return preparer	Class H felony

439. This offense was enacted by S.L. 2017-211, effective for offenses committed on or after January 1, 2018. A fine must be imposed in addition to any other punishment.

Statute	Description of Offense	Punishment
105-236(a)(9b)	Identity theft to make fraudulent submission:[440]	
	To obtain anything of value	Class G felony
	If the person whose identity is stolen suffers adverse financial impact	Class F felony
105-236(a)(10b)	Receiving money from taxpayer and failing to remit to Secretary of Revenue	Class F felony
105-308	Property taxes:	
	Failing to list property	Class 2 misdemeanor
	Attempting to evade tax on property	Class 2 misdemeanor

Chapter 106: Agriculture

106-145.6	Engaging in wholesale distribution without a wholesale distributor license	Class H felony[441]
106-350	Sale of tubercular animal	Class I felony
106-363	Damaging dipping vats	Class H felony
106-549.26	Bribery of or malfeasance of an inspector	Class I felony[442]
106-568.57	Manufacture, deliver, purchase, or possess with intent to manufacture, deliver, purchase, etc., marijuana on property used for hemp production	Class I felony[443]
106-763.1	Possession of an untagged or undocumented alligator	Class H felony
106-942(b), -948	Burning without a permit in or within 500 feet of any woodland in high hazard counties[444]	Class 3 misdemeanor
106-943(b), -948	Burning without a permit in or within 500 feet of any woodland in non–high hazard counties[445]	Class 3 misdemeanor
106-944, -948	Open burning during periods of hazardous forest fire conditions or air pollution episodes	Class 3 misdemeanor

Chapter 108A: Social Services

108A-39(a)	Welfare fraud if value wrongfully received is $400 or less	Class 1 misdemeanor
108A-39(b)	Welfare fraud if value wrongfully received exceeds $400	Class I felony

440. These offenses were enacted by S.L. 2017-204, effective for offenses committed on or after December 1, 2017.
441. The maximum fine for a violation of this offense is $250,000.
442. The punishment for this offense may include a fine of not less than $500 nor more than $10,000.
443. This offense was enacted by S.L. 2016-93, effective for offenses committed on or after December 1, 2016.
444. This offense applies only to the counties of Beaufort, Bladen, Brunswick, Camden, Carteret, Chowan, Craven, Currituck, Dare, Duplin, Gates, Hyde, Jones, Onslow, Pamlico, Pasquotank, Perquimans, Tyrrell, and Washington.
445. This offense applies to counties other than those listed in note 444.

Statute	Description of Offense	Punishment
108A-53(a)	Fraudulently obtaining electronic food and nutrition benefits:	
	If value wrongfully received is $400 or less	Class 1 misdemeanor
	If value wrongfully received exceeds $400	Class I felony
108A-53(b)	Presenting fraudulently obtained electronic food and nutrition benefits	Class 1 misdemeanor
108A-53(c)	Receiving fraudulently obtained electronic food and nutrition benefits	Class 1 misdemeanor
108A-53.1(a)	Unlawful purchase, sale, or distribution of electronic food and nutrition benefits, or possession with intent to sell or distribute	Class H felony
108A-53.1(b)	Unlawful use, transfer, acquisition, alteration, or possession of electronic food and nutrition benefits:	
	If value is less than $100	Class 1 misdemeanor
	If value is $100 to less than $500	Class A1 misdemeanor
	If value is $500 to less than $1,000	Class I felony
	If value is $1,000 or more	Class H felony
108A-57	Withholding information about subrogation rights	Class 1 misdemeanor
108A-63(a), (b), (f), (g), (h)	Medical assistance fraud and related offenses by provider	Class I felony
108A-63(e)	Medical assistance fraud through scheme by provider	Class H felony[446]
108A-64	Medical assistance fraud by recipient:	
	If value wrongfully received is $400 or less	Class 1 misdemeanor
	If value wrongfully received exceeds $400	Class I felony

Chapter 110: Child Welfare

110-107	Child care subsidy fraud:	
	If subsidy is more than $1,000	Class I felony
	If subsidy is $1,000 or less	Class 1 misdemeanor

Chapter 113: Conservation and Development

113-135(a)	Penalties for violating provisions of the marine, estuarine, and wildlife resources subchapter:	
	First conviction	Class 3 misdemeanor
	Subsequent convictions within 3 years	Class 2 misdemeanor

446. The subsection provides that a conspiracy to violate this subsection is a Class I felony.

Statute	Description of Offense	Punishment
113-174.1(a), -135(a)	Recreational fishing without license	Infraction
113-270.1B(a), -135(a)	Fishing without license	Infraction
113-294(e)	Unlawful taking of a deer between a half hour after sunset and a half hour before sunrise with the aid of an artificial light (spotlighting)	Class 2 misdemeanor[447]
113-294(m)	Unlawful taking of any migratory game bird	Class 2 misdemeanor[448]

Chapter 115C: Elementary and Secondary Education

115C-332(h)	Willfully giving false information on public school employment application that is basis for criminal history check	Class A1 misdemeanor
115C-378, -380	Failing to require child to attend school	Class 1 misdemeanor

Chapter 122C: Mental Health, Developmental Disabilities, and Substance Abuse

122C-66(a)	Facility employee or volunteer who causes pain or injury to client	Class A1 misdemeanor
122C-66(a1)	Facility employee or volunteer borrows or takes personal property from client	Class 1 misdemeanor
122C-66(b)	Facility employee or volunteer fails to report violation of G.S. 122C-66(a) or -66(a1) or accidental injury to client	Class 1 misdemeanor
122C-66(b1)	Facility employee or volunteer fails to report when he or she witnesses client become victim of violation of Article 7A or Article 26 of G.S. Chapter 14	Class A1 misdemeanor

Chapter 130A: Public Health

130A-25(a), 14-3(a)	Public health violation other than violation of health control, quarantine, or isolation measures[449]	Class 1 misdemeanor
130A-144(f), -25, 14-3(a)	Violating health control measure	Class 1 misdemeanor[450]

447. This offense is punishable by a fine of not less than $500 in addition to any other punishment prescribed by law.
448. This offense is punishable by a fine of not less than $250 in addition to any other punishment prescribed by law.
449. In addition, violations of Part 7, Article 9, of Chapter 130A and G.S. 130A-309.10(m) are Class 3 misdemeanors.
450. G.S. 130A-25(b) provides that violations of health control, quarantine, or isolation measures or authority under G.S. 130A-144(f) or -145 are not subject to structured sentencing. *See also* G.S. 15A-1340.10 (exempting such violations from structured sentencing). Violating a health control measure is a Class 1 misdemeanor under G.S. 14-3(a), punishable by a term of imprisonment of not more than two years to be served at specified units set out in G.S. 130A-25(b). The person may not be released before completion of the prison term unless the court determines that release would not create a danger to the public health. *See* G.S. 130A-25(b), (c).

Statute	Description of Offense	Punishment
130A-145, -25, 14-3(a)	Violating quarantine or isolation authority	Class 1 misdemeanor[451]
130A-185, -25(a), 14-3(a)	Failure by owner to have dog, cat, or ferret vaccinated against rabies	Class 1 misdemeanor

Chapter 136: Transportation

Statute	Description of Offense	Punishment
136-18(5)	Violating Department of Transportation rules or ordinances	Class 1 misdemeanor
136-26	Roads or highways closed for construction or maintenance:	
	Driving into new construction work	Class 1 misdemeanor
	Removing or damaging barriers, notices, or warning lights	Class 1 misdemeanor
136-90	Obstructing highway	Class 1 misdemeanor
136-91	Placing injurious object on highway or public vehicular area	Class 3 misdemeanor
136-197	Boarding train by intoxicated person after being forbidden by conductor	Class 1 misdemeanor

Chapter 148: State Prison System

Statute	Description of Offense	Punishment
148-45(a)	Escape from state prison system by misdemeanant (first offense)	Class 1 misdemeanor[452]
148-45(b)	Escape from state prison system:[453]	
	By person serving felony sentence or charged with felony and committed to state prison system	Class H felony
	By person previously convicted of escape or attempted escape from state prison system	Class H felony
148-45(d)	Aiding escape from state prison system	Class 1 misdemeanor
148-46.1	Self-injury by prisoner resulting in incapacity to perform assigned work	Class H felony

451. *See supra* note 450.

452. G.S. 148-45(g)(1) provides that failure to return to the custody of the Division of Adult Correction of the Department of Public Safety from work release or other temporary release is treated as escape, punishable under the applicable subsections of G.S. 148-45. *See* State v. Washington, 54 N.C. App. 683 (1981) (although failure to return from work release in violation of subsection (g) of G.S. 148-45 is punishable as escape under subsection (a) or (b), it is a separate offense and must be specifically charged). G.S. 148-45(g)(2) provides that if a person who would otherwise be guilty of a first violation of subsection (g)(1) (failure to return from temporary release) voluntarily returns within 24 hours, he or she shall not be charged with escape. If a person commits a subsequent violation of subsection (g)(1), however, failure to return is an escape even if the person returns within 24 hours.

453. *See supra* note 452.

Appendix A: Crimes Covered under the Crime Victims' Rights Act (CVRA) (G.S. 15A-830)

Felonies

- Any Class A through E felony.
- Abduction of children (G.S. 14-41).
- Assault inflicting serious bodily injury (G.S. 14-32.4).
- Assault on a handicapped person (G.S. 14-32.1(e)).
- Assault on an executive, legislative, or court official with a deadly weapon or inflicting serious injury (G.S. 14-16.6(b)–(c)).
- Assault on emergency personnel with a dangerous weapon or substance (G.S. 14-288.9).
- Assault with a firearm or deadly weapon on a government officer/employee or campus/company police officer (G.S. 14-34.2).
- Assault with a firearm, deadly weapon, or inflicting serious bodily injury on a firefighter, emergency medical technician, or emergency room nurse or physician (G.S. 14-34.6(b)–(c)).
- Common-law robbery (G.S. 14-87.1).
- Domestic abuse or neglect of a disabled or elder adult causing injury or serious injury (G.S. 14-32.3(a)–(b)).
- Felonious restraint (G.S. 14-43.3).
- Habitual impaired driving (G.S. 20-138.5).
- Habitual misdemeanor assault (G.S. 14-33.2).
- Human trafficking of adults (G.S. 14-43.11).
- Involuntary manslaughter (G.S. 14-18).
- Participating in the prostitution of a minor (former G.S. 14-190.19).
- Patient abuse/neglect causing serious bodily injury (G.S. 14-32.2(b)(3)).
- Second-degree arson (G.S. 14-58).
- Second-degree burglary (G.S. 14-51).
- Stalking, second or subsequent offense or when a court order is in effect (G.S. 14-277.3A or former G.S. 14-277.3).
- Taking indecent liberties with children (G.S. 14-202.1).
- Third-degree sexual exploitation of a minor (G.S. 14-190.17A).
- Any attempt of the felonies listed above if the attempt is punishable as a felony.

Misdemeanors

The following apply only when the offense is committed between persons who have a personal relationship as defined in G.S. 50B-1(b). These include: current/former spouse; persons of opposite sex who live or have lived together or who are in or were in a dating relationship; parents/children; grandparents/grandchildren; child in common; current or former household members.

- Assault by pointing a gun (G.S. 14-34).
- Assault inflicting serious injury or using a deadly weapon (G.S. 14-33(c)(1)).
- Assault on a female (G.S. 14-33(c)(2)).
- Domestic criminal trespass (G.S. 14-134.3).
- Simple assault or affray (G.S. 14-33(a)).
- Stalking, first offense (G.S. 14-277.3A or former G.S. 14-277.3).

Protective Order Violations

- Any violation of a valid protective order under G.S. 50B-4.1.

Appendix B: Crimes Requiring Sex Offender Registration (G.S. 14-208.6)

Sexually Violent Offenses (G.S. 14-208.6(5))

First-Degree Forcible Rape (G.S. 14-27.21)	Committed on/after 12/1/2015
Second-Degree Forcible Rape (G.S. 14-27.22)	Committed on/after 12/1/2015
Statutory Rape of a Child by an Adult (G.S. 14-27.23)	Committed on/after 12/1/2015
First-Degree Statutory Rape (G.S. 14-27.24)	Effective 12/1/2015
Statutory Rape of Person ≤ 15yo/D 6+ Years Older (G.S. 14-27.25(a))	Committed on/after 12/1/2015
First-Degree Forcible Sexual Offense (G.S. 14-27.26)	Committed on/after 12/1/2015
Second-Degree Forcible Sexual Offense (G.S. 14-27.27)	Committed on/after 12/1/2015
Statutory Sexual Offense with a Child by an Adult (G.S. 14-27.28)	Committed on/after 12/1/2015
First-Degree Statutory Sexual Offense (G.S. 14-27.29)	Committed on/after 12/1/2015
Statutory Sexual Offense with Person ≤ 15yo/D 6+ Years Older (G.S. 14-27.30(a))	Committed on/after 12/1/2015
Sexual Activity by a Substitute Parent or Custodian (G.S. 14-27.31)	Committed on/after 12/1/2015
Sexual Activity with a Student (G.S. 14-27.32)	Committed on/after 12/1/2015
Sexual Battery (G.S. 14-27.33)	Committed on/after 12/1/2015
Human Trafficking (*Only if Victim < 18 or for Sex Servitude*) (G.S. 14-43.11)	Committed on/after 12/1/2013
Sexual Servitude (G.S. 14-43.13)	Committed on/after 12/1/2006
Incest between Near Relatives (G.S. 14-178)	Convicted/released from prison on/after 1/1/1996
Employ Minor in Offense/Public Morality (G.S. 14-190.6)	Convicted/released from prison on/after 1/1/1996
Felony Indecent Exposure (G.S. 14-190.9(a1))	Committed on/after 12/1/2005
First-Degree Sexual Exploitation of Minor (G.S. 14-190.16)	Convicted/released from prison on/after 1/1/1996
Second-Degree Sexual Exploitation of Minor (G.S. 14-190.17)	Convicted/released from prison on/after 1/1/1996
Third-Degree Sexual Exploitation of Minor (G.S. 14-190.17A)	Convicted/released from prison on/after 1/1/1996
Taking Indecent Liberties with Children (G.S. 14-202.1)	Convicted/released from prison on/after 1/1/1996
Solicitation of Child by Computer (G.S. 14-202.3)	Committed on/after 12/1/2005
Taking Indecent Liberties with a Student (G.S. 14-202.4(a))	Convicted/released from prison on/after 12/1/2009
Patronizing Minor/Mentally Disabled Prostitute (G.S. 14-205.2(c)–(d))	Committed on/after 10/1/2013
Prostitution of Minor/Mentally Disabled Child (G.S. 14-205.3(b))	Committed on/after 10/1/2013
Parent/Caretaker Prostitution (G.S. 14-318.4(a1))	Convicted/released from prison on/after 12/1/2008
Parent/Guardian Commit/Allow Sexual Act (G.S. 14-318.4(a2))	Convicted/released from prison on/after 12/1/2008
Former First-Degree Rape (G.S. 14-27.2)	Convicted/released from prison on/after 1/1/1996
Former Rape of a Child by an Adult Offender (G.S. 14-27.2A)	Committed on/after 12/1/2008
Former Second-Degree Rape (G.S. 14-27.3)	Convicted/released from prison on/after 1/1/1996
Former First-Degree Sexual Offense (G.S. 14-27.4)	Convicted/released from prison on/after 1/1/1996
Former Sexual Offense with a Child by an Adult Offender (G.S. 14-27.4A)	Committed on/after 12/1/2008
Former Second-Degree Sexual Offense (G.S. 14-27.5)	Convicted/released from prison on/after 1/1/1996
Former Sexual Battery (G.S. 14-27.5A)	Committed on/after 12/1/2005
Former Attempted Rape/Sexual Offense (G.S. 14-27.6)	Convicted/released from prison on/after 1/1/1996
Former Intercourse/Sexual Offense w/Certain Victims (G.S. 14-27.7)	Convicted/released from prison on/after 1/1/1996
Former Statutory Rape/Sexual Offense (13–15yo/D 6+ Years Older) (G.S. 14-27.7A(a))	Committed on/after 12/1/2006
Former Promoting Prostitution of Minor (G.S. 14-190.18)	Convicted/released from prison on/after 1/1/1996
Former Participating in Prostitution of Minor (G.S. 14-190.19)	Convicted/released from prison on/after 1/1/1996

Offenses Against a Minor (G.S. 14-208.6(1m))—Reportable Only When Victim Is a Minor and the Offender Is Not the Minor's Parent

Kidnapping (G.S. 14-39)	Committed on/after 4/1/1998 (at a minimum)
Abduction of Children (G.S. 14-41)	Committed on/after 4/1/1998 (at a minimum)
Felonious Restraint (G.S. 14-43.3)	Committed on/after 4/1/1998 (at a minimum)

Peeping Crimes (G.S. 14-208.6(4)d.)—Reportable Only if the Court Decides That Registration Furthers Purposes of the Registry and That the Offender Is a Danger to Community

Felony Peeping under G.S. 14-202(d), (e), (f), (g), or (h)	Committed on/after 12/1/2003
or Second/Subsequent Conviction of:	
Misdemeanor Peeping under G.S. 14-202(a) or (c)	Committed on/after 12/1/2003
Misdemeanor Peeping w/Mirror/Device under G.S. 14-202(a1)	Committed on/after 12/1/2004

Sale of a Child (G.S. 14-208.6(4)e.). Reportable only if the sentencing court rules under G.S. 14-43.14(e) that the person is a danger to the community and required to register. (*Offenses committed on/after 12/1/2012.*)

Attempt. Final convictions for attempts to commit an "offense against a minor" or a "sexually violent offense" are reportable. G.S. 14-208.6(4)a. (*Offenses committed on/after 4/1/1998*, at a minimum, unless target offense has later effective date.)

Conspiracy/Solicitation. Conspiracy and solicitation to commit an "offense against a minor" or a "sexually violent offense" are reportable. G.S. 14-208.6(1m); -208.6(5). (*Offenses committed on/after 12/1/1999*, unless underlying offense has a later effective date.)

Aiding and Abetting. Aiding and abetting an "offense against a minor" or "sexually violent offense" is reportable only if the court finds that registration furthers the purposes of the registry (set out in G.S. 14-208.5). G.S. 14-208.6(4)a. (*Offenses committed on/after 12/1/1999*, unless underlying offense has a later effective date.)

Appendix C: Conviction-Based Driver's License Revocations

Shea Riggsbee Denning

Conviction Statute	Offense Description	Revocation Statute	Length of Revocation	Number of Restorations	Alcohol Concentration Restriction under G.S. 20-19(c3)	Duration of G.S. 20-19(c3) Alcohol Concentration Restriction	Ignition Interlock (II) and Alcohol Concentration (AC) Restriction under G.S. 20-17.8	Length of Ignition Interlock Restriction
G.S. 14-31	Secret assault with a deadly weapon using a motor vehicle	G.S. 20-17(a)(11)	1 year; G.S. 20-19(f)					
G.S. 14-32(a)	Assault with a deadly weapon with intent to kill, inflicting serious injury using a motor vehicle	G.S. 20-17(a)(11)	1 year; G.S. 20-19(f)					
G.S. 14-32(b)	Assault with a deadly weapon, inflicting serious injury using a motor vehicle	G.S. 20-17(a)(11)	1 year; G.S. 20-19(f)					
G.S. 14-32(c)	Assault with a deadly weapon with intent to kill using a motor vehicle	G.S. 20-17(a)(11)	1 year; G.S. 20-19(f)					
G.S. 14-32.1(e)(1)	Assault with a deadly weapon on a handicapped person using a motor vehicle	G.S. 20-17(a)(11)	1 year; G.S. 20-19(f)					
G.S. 14-33(c)(1)	Assault with a deadly weapon using a motor vehicle	G.S. 20-17(a)(11)	1 year; G.S. 20-19(f)					
G.S. 14-49(b),(b1)	Malicious use of an explosive device to damage property	G.S. 20-17(a)(15); G.S. 20-13.2(c2) (applicable to persons under 18)	1 year; G.S. 20-19(f); G.S. 20-13.2(d) (applicable to persons under 18)					
G.S. 14-69.1(c)	False report of a bomb in a public building	G.S. 20-17(a)(15); G.S. 20-13.2(c2) (applicable to persons under 18)	1 year; G.S. 20-19(f); G.S. 20-13.2(d) (applicable to persons under 18)					
G.S. 14-69.2(c)	Perpetrating a hoax concerning a bomb in a public building	G.S. 20-17(a)(15); G.S. 20-13.2(c2) (applicable to persons under 18)	1 year; G.S. 20-19(f); G.S. 20-13.2(d) (applicable to persons under 18)					

Conviction Statute	Offense Description	Revocation Statute	Length of Revocation	Number of Restorations	Alcohol Concentration Restriction under G.S. 20-19(c3)	Duration of G.S. 20-19(c3) Alcohol Concentration Restriction	Ignition Interlock (II) and Alcohol Concentration (AC) Restriction under G.S. 20-17.8	Length of Ignition Interlock Restriction
G.S. 14-72.5	Second or subsequent conviction (within 7 years) of larceny of motor fuel	G.S. 20-17(a)(16)	90 days (second conviction); 6 months (third or subsequent conviction); G.S. 20-19(g2)					
G.S. 14-269.2(b1)	Possessing an explosive on educational property	G.S. 20-17(a)(15); G.S. 20-13.2(c2) (applicable to persons under 18)	1 year; G.S. 20-19(f); G.S. 20-13.2(d) (applicable to persons under 18)					
G.S. 14-269.2(c1)	Causing a minor to possess an explosive on educational property	G.S. 20-17(a)(15); G.S. 20-13.2(c2) (applicable to persons under 18)	1 year; G.S. 20-19(f); G.S. 20-13.2(d) (applicable to persons under 18)					
G.S. 18B-302(a1)	Giving alcoholic beverages to person under 21	G.S. 20-17.3	1 year; G.S. 20-17.3					
G.S. 18B-302(b)	Underage purchase or attempt to purchase an alcoholic beverage	G.S. 20-17.3	1 year; G.S. 20-17.3					
G.S. 18B-302(c)(1)	Underage person who aids or abets the gift or purchase of an alcoholic beverage to/by a minor[1]	G.S. 20-17.3	1 year; G.S. 20-17.3					
G.S. 18B-302(c)(2)	Person over 21 who aids or abets the gift or purchase of an alcoholic beverage to/by a minor	G.S. 20-17.3	1 year; G.S. 20-17.3					

1. G.S. 20-17.3 requires DMV to revoke for one year the driver's license of a person convicted of violating G.S. 18B-302(c). G.S. 18B-302(c) in turn renders it unlawful to aid or abet another in a violation of G.S. 18B-302(a), (a1), or (b). G.S. 18B-302(g) requires the court to file a conviction report with DMV if the person is convicted of a violation of G.S. 18B-302(a1); 18B-302(b), but only if the violation occurred while the person was purchasing or attempting to purchase an alcoholic beverage; or 18B-302(c), (e), or (f). Thus, it appears that a person's license may be revoked for aiding and abetting the gift to or purchase of alcoholic beverages to/by an underage person but not for sale to an underage person (prohibited by G.S. 18B-302(a)) or consumption by an underage person (prohibited by G.S. 18B-302(b)(3)).

Conviction Statute	Offense Description	Revocation Statute	Length of Revocation	Number of Restorations	Alcohol Concentration Restriction under G.S. 20-19(c3)	Duration of G.S. 20-19(c3) Alcohol Concentration Restriction	Ignition Interlock (II) and Alcohol Concentration (AC) Restriction under G.S. 20-17.8	Length of Ignition Interlock Restriction
G.S. 18B-302(e)	Fraudulent use of identification • to enter or attempt to enter a place where alcoholic beverages are sold or consumed • to obtain or attempt to obtain an alcoholic beverage • to obtain or attempt to obtain permission to purchase alcoholic beverages	G.S. 20-17.3	1 year; G.S. 20-17.3					
G.S. 18B-302(f)	Allowing use of identification by a person who violates or attempts to violate G.S. 18B-302(b)	G.S. 20-17.3	1 year; G.S. 20-17.3					
G.S. 18B-401	Transportation of an open bottle of fortified wine or spirituous liquor in passenger area	Discretionary revocation: G.S. 20-16(a)(8)	Not more than 6 months; G.S. 20-19(a)					
G.S. 18B-406	Transportation of unauthorized amount of alcoholic beverage	Discretionary revocation: G.S. 20-16(a)(8)	Not more than 6 months; G.S. 20-19(a)					
G.S. 18B-111	Transportation of a nontaxpaid alcoholic beverage	Discretionary revocation: G.S. 20-16(a)(8)	Not more than 6 months; G.S. 20-19(a)					
G.S. 20-12.1	Impaired instruction	Discretionary revocation: G.S. 20-16(a)(8a)	Not more than 1 year; G.S. 20-19(c)					

Conviction Statute	Offense Description	Revocation Statute	Length of Revocation	Number of Restorations	Alcohol Concentration Restriction under G.S. 20-19(c3)	Duration of G.S. 20-19(c3) Alcohol Concentration Restriction	Ignition Interlock (II) and Alcohol Concentration (AC) Restriction under G.S. 20-17.8	Length of Ignition Interlock Restriction
G.S. 20-28(a) (2014) *Note:* Convictions under this provision result in license revocation if the offense was committed before December 1, 2015. For offenses committed December 1, 2015, or later, a conviction under G.S. 20-28(a) does not trigger an additional period of revocation.	Driving while license revoked	G.S. 20-28(a) (2014)	For offenses committed before December 1, 2015: First offense: 1 year; Second offense: 2 years; Third or subsequent offense: Permanent; G.S. 20-28(a) (2014)					
G.S. 20-28(a1)	Driving while license revoked for impaired driving	G.S. 20-28(a1)	First offense: 1 year; Second offense: 2 years Third or subsequent offense: Permanent; G.S. 20-28(a1)					
G.S. 20-28(a2) (2014) *Note:* This provision was recodified for offenses committed on or after December 1, 2015. Thus, only persons convicted under this provision for offenses committed before December 1, 2015, are subject to license revocation.	Driving after notification or failure to appear	G.S. 20-28(a2) (2014)	For offenses committed before December 1, 2015: First offense: 1 year; Second offense: 2 years; Third or subsequent offense: Permanent; G.S. 20-28(a2) (2014)					
G.S. 20-28(a3)	Driving after notification or failure to appear	G.S. 20-28(a3)	First offense: 1 year; Second offense: 2 years Third or subsequent offense: Permanent; G.S. 20-28(a3)					

Conviction Statute	Offense Description	Revocation Statute	Length of Revocation	Number of Restorations	Alcohol Concentration Restriction under G.S. 20-19(c3)	Duration of G.S. 20-19(c3) Alcohol Concentration Restriction	Ignition Interlock (II) and Alcohol Concentration (AC) Restriction under G.S. 20-17.8	Length of Ignition Interlock Restriction
G.S. 20-28(d)	Driving a commercial motor vehicle during disqualification	G.S. 20-28(d) provides for an additional disqualification period—not revocation of a regular license; surrender of Class C license is not required (G.S. 20-24(a))						
G.S. 20-28.1	Moving violation while license revoked	G.S. 20-28.1	First revocation: 1 year; Second revocation: 2 years; Third or subsequent revocation: Permanent; G.S. 20-28.1(b)					
G.S. 20-30(1)	Displaying or possessing any license or learner's permit known to be invalid	Discretionary revocation: G.S. 20-16(a)(6)	Not more than 1 year; G.S. 20-19(c)					
G.S. 20-30(2)	Counterfeiting, selling, lending, or knowingly permitting the use of any driver's license or learner's permit by one not entitled thereto	Discretionary revocation: G.S. 20-16(a)(6)	Not more than 1 year; G.S. 20-19(c)					
G.S. 20-30(3)	Displaying or representing as one's own a license not issued to the person displaying it	Discretionary revocation: G.S. 20-16(a)(6)	Not more than 1 year; G.S. 20-19(c)					
G.S. 20-30(5)	Using or allowing others to use false names and addresses in license applications and renewals	G.S. 20-17(a)(8)[2]	1 year; G.S. 20-19(f)					

2. If a person falsely certifies to DMV pursuant to G.S. 20-9(i)(3) that he or she does not appear on the National Sex Offender Public Registry, that person violates G.S. 20-30 and DMV must immediately revoke his or her driver's license upon determining that the person does appear in the National Sex Offender Public Registry. G.S. 20-9(i)(3).

Conviction Statute	Offense Description	Revocation Statute	Length of Revocation	Number of Restorations	Alcohol Concentration Restriction under G.S. 20-19(c3)	Duration of G.S. 20-19(c3) Alcohol Concentration Restriction	Ignition Interlock (II) and Alcohol Concentration (AC) Restriction under G.S. 20-17.8	Length of Ignition Interlock Restriction
G.S. 20-30(5)	Making false statements, concealing material facts, or otherwise committing a fraud in applying for a license or permit	G.S. 20-17(a)(8)	1 year; G.S. 20-19(f)					
G.S. 20-31	Making a false affidavit or knowingly swearing or affirming falsely to any matter or thing required by the statutes to be sworn to	G.S. 20-17(a)(5); G.S. 20-17(a)(8)	1 year; G.S. 20-19(f)					
G.S. 20-136	Unlawful possession of a motor vehicle with smoke screens	G.S. 20-17(a)(3)	1 year; G.S. 20-19(f)					
G.S. 20-138.1	Impaired driving	G.S. 20-17(a)(2)	1 year; G.S. 20-19(c1)	First restoration	0.04	3 years	If alcohol concentration of 0.15 or more, II required with 0.04 AC restriction.[3] If convicted of another impaired driving offense that occurred within 7 years of current offense, II required with 0.00 AC restriction.	1 year
G.S. 20-138.1	Impaired driving and the person has been convicted of another offense involving impaired driving that occurred within 3 years preceding the date of the current offense	G.S. 20-17(a)(2)	4 years; G.S. 20-19(d)	Second or subsequent restoration	0.00	3 years	II required, 0.00 AC	3 years

3. If ignition interlock is required because the person had an alcohol concentration of 0.15 or more and the person also is convicted, based on the same set of circumstances, of (1) driving while impaired in a commercial vehicle in violation of G.S. 20-138.2, (2) driving while less than 21 years old after consuming alcohol or drugs in violation of G.S. 20-138.3, (3) death or serious injury by vehicle in violation of G.S. 20-141.4, or (4) manslaughter or negligent homicide based on impaired driving, the restriction must prohibit driving with an alcohol concentration of greater than 0.00. G.S. 20-17.8(b)(3)c.

Conviction Statute	Offense Description	Revocation Statute	Length of Revocation	Number of Restorations	Alcohol Concentration Restriction under G.S. 20-19(c3)	Duration of G.S. 20-19(c3) Alcohol Concentration Restriction	Ignition Interlock (II) and Alcohol Concentration (AC) Restriction under G.S. 20-17.8	Length of Ignition Interlock Restriction
G.S. 20-138.1	Impaired driving and the person has two or more previous offenses for which he or she has been convicted, one of which occurred within the 5 years immediately preceding the date of the current offense	G.S. 20-17(a)(2)	Permanent; G.S. 20-19(e)	Second or subsequent restoration	0.00	7 years	II required, 0.00 AC	7 years
G.S. 20-138.1	Impaired driving sentenced at Aggravated Level One pursuant to G.S. 20-179(f3)	G.S. 20-17(a)(2)	Permanent; G.S. 20-19(e)	First restoration	0.04	7 years	II required, 0.00 AC	1 year
G.S. 20-138.1	Impaired driving sentenced at Aggravated Level One pursuant to G.S. 20-179(f3)	G.S. 20-17(a)(2)	Permanent; G.S. 20-19(e)	Second or subsequent restoration	0.00	7 years	II required, 0.00 AC	7 years
	Out-of-state or federal DWI	G.S. 20-23; G.S. 20-23.2	1 year	First restoration	0.04	3 years	No II Requirement	N/A
	Out-of-state or federal DWI and the person has been convicted of another offense involving impaired driving that occurred within the 3 years preceding the date of the current offense	G.S. 20-23; G.S. 20-23.2	4 years	Second or subsequent restoration	0.00	3 years	No II Requirement	N/A
	Out-of-state or federal DWI and the person has two or more previous offenses for which he or she has been convicted, one of which occurred within the 5 years immediately preceding the date of the current offense	G.S. 20-23; G.S. 20-23.2	Permanent	Second or subsequent restoration	0.00	7 years	No II Requirement	N/A

Conviction Statute	Offense Description	Revocation Statute	Length of Revocation	Number of Restorations	Alcohol Concentration Restriction under G.S. 20-19(c3)	Duration of G.S. 20-19(c3) Alcohol Concentration Restriction	Ignition Interlock (II) and Alcohol Concentration (AC) Restriction under G.S. 20-17.8	Length of Ignition Interlock Restriction
G.S. 20-138.2	Driving a commercial motor vehicle while impaired with alcohol concentration of 0.06 or higher and person has been convicted of another offense involving impaired driving that occurred within 3 years preceding date of current offense	G.S. 20-17(a)(2)	4 years	Any restoration	0.00	3 years	No II Requirement	N/A
G.S. 20-138.2	Driving a commercial motor vehicle while impaired with alcohol concentration of 0.06 or higher and the person has 2 or more previous offenses for which he or she has been convicted, one of which occurred within the 5 years immediately preceding the date of the current offense	G.S. 20-17(a)(2)	Permanent; G.S. 20-19(e)	Any restoration	0.00	7 years	No II Requirement	N/A
G.S. 20-138.2	Driving a commercial motor vehicle while impaired with an alcohol concentration of 0.06 or higher sentenced at Aggravated Level One pursuant to G.S. 20-179(f3)	G.S. 20-17(a)(2)	Permanent; G.S. 20-19(e)	Any restoration	0.00	7 years	No II Requirement	N/A
	Out-of-state or federal DWI in a commercial motor vehicle with alcohol concentration of 0.06 or higher	G.S. 20-23; G.S. 20-23.2	1 year	Any restoration	0.00	3 years	No II Requirement	N/A

Conviction Statute	Offense Description	Revocation Statute	Length of Revocation	Number of Restorations	Alcohol Concentration Restriction under G.S. 20-19(c3)	Duration of G.S. 20-19(c3) Alcohol Concentration Restriction	Ignition Interlock (II) and Alcohol Concentration (AC) Restriction under G.S. 20-17.8	Length of Ignition Interlock Restriction
	Out-of-state or federal DWI in a commercial motor vehicle with alcohol concentration of 0.06 or higher and the person has been convicted of another offense involving impaired driving that occurred within the 3 years preceding the date of the current offense	G.S. 20-23; G.S. 20-23.2	4 years	Any restoration	0.00	3 years	No II Requirement	N/A
	Out-of-state or federal DWI in a commercial motor vehicle with alcohol concentration of 0.06 or higher and the person has 2 or more previous offenses for which he or she has been convicted, 1 of which occurred within the 5 years immediately preceding the date of the current offense	G.S. 20-23; G.S. 20-23.2	Permanent	Any restoration	0.00	7 years	No II Requirement	N/A
G.S. 20-138.2A	Second or subsequent conviction (within 7 years) of driving a commercial motor vehicle after consuming alcohol	G.S. 20-17(a)(13)	1 year; G.S. 20-19(f)					
G.S. 20-138.2B	Driving a school bus, school activity bus, child care vehicle, ambulance or other EMS vehicle, firefighting vehicle, or law enforcement vehicle after consuming alcohol	G.S. 20-17(a)(14)	First conviction: 10 days; Second or subsequent conviction: 1 year; G.S. 20-19(c2)					
G.S. 20-138.3	Driving after consuming alcohol or drugs by a person under 21	G.S. 20-13.2	1 year; G.S. 20-13.2(d)	Any restoration	0.00	Until the person is 21	No II Requirement	N/A

Conviction Statute	Offense Description	Revocation Statute	Length of Revocation	Number of Restorations	Alcohol Concentration Restriction under G.S. 20-19(c3)	Duration of G.S. 20-19(c3) Alcohol Concentration Restriction	Ignition Interlock (II) and Alcohol Concentration (AC) Restriction under G.S. 20-17.8	Length of Ignition Interlock Restriction
G.S. 20-138.5	Habitual impaired driving	G.S. 20-138.5(d)	Permanent; G.S. 20-138.5(d)	Any restoration	0.00	7 years	No II Requirement	N/A
G.S. 20-138.7	Second or subsequent conviction of transporting an open container of alcoholic beverage under G.S. 20-138.7	G.S. 20-17(a)(12)	1 year; G.S. 20-19(f)					
G.S. 20-140 (reckless driving); G.S. 20-141.6 (aggressive driving)	Conviction within 12 months of (1) 2 charges of reckless driving, (2) 2 charges of aggressive driving, or (3) 1 or more charges of reckless driving and 1 or more charges of aggressive driving	G.S. 20-17(a)(6)	1 year; G.S. 20-19(f)					
G.S. 20-140 (reckless driving); G.S. 20-141.6 (aggressive driving)	Conviction of 1 charge of aggressive driving or reckless driving while engaged in illegal transportation of intoxicants for sale	G.S. 20-17(a)(7)	1 year; G.S. 20-19(f)					
G.S. 20-141	Speeding over 15 m.p.h. over limit and over 55 m.p.h. (includes work zone charges) or over 80 m.p.h.	G.S. 20-16.1	30-day suspension for first offense; 60-day suspension for second offense; G.S. 20-16.1(a), (c)					
G.S. 20-141	Speeding over 15 m.p.h. over limit and over 55 m.p.h. (includes work zone charges) or over 80 m.p.h. and reckless driving (G.S. 20-140)	G.S. 20-16.1	60-day suspension for second offense; G.S. 20-16.1(d)					
G.S. 20-141	Conviction within 12 months of 2 or more charges of speeding more than 55 m.p.h. and not more than 80 m.p.h.	Discretionary revocation: G.S. 20-16(a)(9)	Not more than 6 months; G.S. 20-19(a)					

Conviction Statute	Offense Description	Revocation Statute	Length of Revocation	Number of Restorations	Alcohol Concentration Restriction under G.S. 20-19(c3)	Duration of G.S. 20-19(c3) Alcohol Concentration Restriction	Ignition Interlock (II) and Alcohol Concentration (AC) Restriction under G.S. 20-17.8	Length of Ignition Interlock Restriction
G.S. 20-141; G.S. 20-140	Conviction within 12 months of 1 or more charges of reckless driving and 1 or more charges of speeding in excess of 55 m.p.h. and not more than 80 m.p.h.	Discretionary revocation: G.S. 20-16(a)(9)	Not more than 6 months; G.S. 20-19(a)					
G.S. 20-141; G.S. 20-141.6	Conviction within 12 months of 1 or more charges of aggressive driving and 1 or more charges of speeding in excess of 55 m.p.h. and not more than 80 m.p.h.	Discretionary revocation: G.S. 20-16(a)(9)	Not more than 6 months; G.S. 20-19(a)					
G.S. 20-141	Conviction of speeding more than 75 m.p.h. where speed limit is less than 70 m.p.h.	Discretionary revocation: G.S. 20-16(a)(10)	Not more than 12 months; G.S. 20-19(b)					
G.S. 20-141	Conviction of speeding more than 80 m.p.h. where speed limit is 70 m.p.h.	Discretionary revocation: G.S. 20-16(a)(10a)	Not more than 1 year; G.S. 20-19(c)					
G.S. 20-141.3(a)	Engaging in a prearranged speed competition with another motor vehicle	G.S. 20-141.3(d)	3 years; person may apply for new license after 18 months; G.S. 20-141.3(d)					
G.S. 20-141.3(b)	Willfully engaging in a speed competition with another motor vehicle (not prearranged)	Discretionary revocation: G.S. 20-141.3(e)	Up to 1 year; G.S. 20-141.3(e)					
G.S. 20-141.3(c)	Allowing or authorizing others to use one's motor vehicle in a prearranged speed competition	G.S. 20-141.3(d)	3 years; person may apply for a new license after 18 months; G.S. 20-141.3(d)					
G.S. 20-141.3(c)	Placing or receiving a bet or wager on a prearranged speed competition	G.S. 20-141.3(d)	3 years; person may apply for a new license after 18 months; G.S. 20-141.3(d)					
G.S. 20-141.4	Misdemeanor death by vehicle	G.S. 20-17(a)(9)	1 year; G.S. 20-19(f)					

Conviction Statute	Offense Description	Revocation Statute	Length of Revocation	Number of Restorations	Alcohol Concentration Restriction under G.S. 20-19(c3)	Duration of G.S. 20-19(c3) Alcohol Concentration Restriction	Ignition Interlock (II) and Alcohol Concentration (AC) Restriction under G.S. 20-17.8	Length of Ignition Interlock Restriction
G.S. 20-141.4(a1)	Felony death by vehicle	G.S. 20-17(a)(9)	Permanent; G.S. 20-19(i)	Any restoration	0.00	7 years	No II Requirement	N/A
	Out-of-state felony death by vehicle	G.S. 20-23; G.S. 20-23.2	Permanent	Any restoration	0.00	7 years	No II Requirement	N/A
G.S. 20-141.4(a3)	Felony serious injury by vehicle	G.S. 20-17(a)(9)	4 years; G.S. 20-19(d)	Unclear[4]	Unclear[5]	3 years	No II Requirement	N/A
	Out-of-state felony serious injury by vehicle	G.S. 20-23; G.S. 20-23.2	4 years	Any restoration	0.00	3 years	No II Requirement	N/A
G.S. 20-141.4(a4)	Aggravated felony serious injury by vehicle	G.S. 20-17(a)(9)	Permanent; G.S. 20-19(e)	Unclear[6]	Unclear[7]	7 years	No II Requirement	N/A
	Out-of-state or federal felony serious injury by vehicle	G.S. 20-23; G.S. 20-23.2	Permanent	Any restoration	0.00	7 years	No II Requirement	N/A
G.S. 20-141.4(a5)	Aggravated felony death by vehicle	G.S. 20-17(a)(9)	Permanent; G.S. 20-19(i)	Any restoration[8]	0.00	7 years	No II Requirement	N/A
	Out-of-state or federal felony death by vehicle	G.S. 20-17(a)(9)	Permanent	Any restoration	0.00	7 years	No II Requirement	N/A
G.S. 20-141.4(a6)	Repeat felony death by vehicle	G.S. 20-17(a)(9)	Permanent; G.S. 20-19(i)	Any restoration[9]	0.00	7 years	No II Requirement	N/A
	Out-of-state or federal repeat or felony death by vehicle	G.S. 20-23; G.S. 20-23.2	Permanent	Any restoration	0.00	7 years	No II Requirement	N/A

4. No alcohol concentration restriction is specified by statute for license restorations following convictions of felony serious injury by vehicle under G.S. 20-141.4(a3). In contrast, G.S. 20-19(c3)(4) imposes an alcohol concentration restriction of 0.00 for any license restored following a revocation for an out-of-state or federal conviction of an offense that is substantially similar to a violation of G.S. 20-141.4—the statute that defines both death by vehicle and serious injury by vehicle offenses.

5. *See supra* note 4.

6. *See supra* note 4.

7. *See supra* note 4.

8. G.S. 20-19(c3)(3) requires an alcohol concentration restriction of 0.00 for any restoration for a person convicted of "felony death by vehicle, G.S. 20-141.4(a1), [or] manslaughter or negligent homicide resulting from the operation of a motor vehicle when the offense involved impaired driving." Given that felony death by vehicle is a lesser-included offense of aggravated felony death by vehicle, it seems beyond dispute that these restrictions apply to persons convicted of the greater offense.

9. G.S. 20-19(c3)(3) requires an alcohol concentration restriction of 0.00 for any restoration for a person convicted of "felony death by vehicle, G.S. 20-141.4(a1), [or] manslaughter or negligent homicide resulting from the operation of a motor vehicle when the offense involved impaired driving." Given that felony death by vehicle is a lesser-included offense of repeat felony death by vehicle, it seems beyond dispute that these restrictions apply to persons convicted of the greater offense.

Conviction Statute	Offense Description	Revocation Statute	Length of Revocation	Number of Restorations	Alcohol Concentration Restriction under G.S. 20-19(c3)	Duration of G.S. 20-19(c3) Alcohol Concentration Restriction	Ignition Interlock (II) and Alcohol Concentration (AC) Restriction under G.S. 20-17.8	Length of Ignition Interlock Restriction
Common law offense	Involuntary manslaughter resulting from the operation of a motor vehicle	G.S. 20-17(a)(1)	Permanent; G.S. 20-19(i)	Any restoration	0.00	7 years	No II requirement	N/A
	Out-of-state or federal conviction for involuntary manslaughter resulting from the operation of a motor vehicle	G.S. 20-23; G.S. 20-23.2	Permanent	Any restoration	0.00	7 years	No II requirement	N/A
G.S. 20-141.5(a)	Misdemeanor speeding to elude arrest	G.S. 20-141.5(d)	Not more than 1 year; G.S. 20-141.5(d)					
G.S. 20-141.5(b)	Felony speeding to elude arrest (Class H felony)	G.S. 20-141.5(d)	2 years if 2 aggravating factors under G.S. 20-141.5(b); 3 years if 3 or more aggravating factors; G.S. 20-141.5(d)					
G.S. 20-141.5(b1)	Misdemeanor speeding to elude arrest that causes death (Class H felony)	G.S. 20-141.5(d)	2 years if 2 aggravating factors under G.S. 20-141.5(b); 3 years if 3 or more aggravating factors; G.S. 20-141.5(d)					
G.S. 20-141.5(b1)	Felony speeding to elude arrest that causes death (Class E felony)	G.S. 20-141.5(d)	2 years if 2 aggravating factors under G.S. 20-141.5(b); 3 years if 3 or more aggravating factors; G.S. 20-141.5(d)					
G.S. 20-154(a2)	Unsafe movement resulting in a crash causing property damage of more than $5,000 or serious bodily injury to a motorcycle operator or passenger	Discretionary revocation: G.S. 20-154(a2) (in discretion of trial court rather than DMV)	Not more than 30 days; G.S. 20-154(a2)					

Conviction Statute	Offense Description	Revocation Statute	Length of Revocation	Number of Restorations	Alcohol Concentration Restriction under G.S. 20-19(c3)	Duration of G.S. 20-19(c3) Alcohol Concentration Restriction	Ignition Interlock (II) and Alcohol Concentration (AC) Restriction under G.S. 20-17.8	Length of Ignition Interlock Restriction
G.S. 20-157(i)	Failure to stop for approaching fire, police, rescue vehicle, etc., or other violation of G.S. 20-157 that causes serious injury or death	Discretionary revocation: G.S. 20-157(i)	Not more than 6 months; G.S. 20-157(i)					
G.S. 20-160.1	Failure to yield resulting in serious bodily injury	G.S. 20-160.1	90 days; G.S. 20-160.1(a).					
G.S. 20-166(a), (a1)	Failure to stop or remain with vehicle involved in injury crash	G.S. 20-17(a)(4) (applicable to convictions for failure to stop under G.S. 20-166(a)); G.S. 20-166(e) (applicable to convictions under G.S. 20-166(a) or (a1))	1 year, unless the court finds that a longer period of revocation is appropriate, in which case revocation is for 2 years; G.S. 20-166(e)					
G.S. 20-166(b)	Failure to render aid to a person injured in a crash	G.S. 20-17(a)(4)	1 year; G.S. 20-19(f)					
G.S. 20-217(a) Offenses committed on or after December 1, 2013	Second conviction within 3 years of misdemeanor violation of G.S. 20-217 (passing stopped school bus)	G.S. 20-217(g1) [10]	1 year; G.S. 20-217(g1)					
G.S. 20-217(a) Offenses committed on or after December 1, 2013	Third conviction of misdemeanor violation of G.S. 20-217 (passing stopped school bus)	G.S. 20-217(g1) [11]	Permanent; G.S. 20-217(g1)					
G.S. 20-217(g)	Passing stopped school bus and striking person (Class I felony)	G.S. 20-17(a)(3) [12]	1 year; G.S. 20-19(f)					
G.S. 20-217(g) Offenses committed on or after December 1, 2013	Passing stopped school bus and striking person (Class I felony)	G.S. 20-217(g1) [13]	2 years; G.S. 20-217(g1)					

10. Effective for offenses committed on or after December 1, 2013.
11. *See supra* note 10.
12. Requiring revocation upon conviction of a felony in the commission of which a motor vehicle is used.
13. *See supra* note 10.

Conviction Statute	Offense Description	Revocation Statute	Length of Revocation	Number of Restorations	Alcohol Concentration Restriction under G.S. 20-19(c3)	Duration of G.S. 20-19(c3) Alcohol Concentration Restriction	Ignition Interlock (II) and Alcohol Concentration (AC) Restriction under G.S. 20-17.8	Length of Ignition Interlock Restriction
G.S. 20-217(g)	Passing a stopped school bus and striking a person, causing death (Class H felony)	G.S. 20-17(a)(3) [14]	1 year; G.S. 20-217(g1)					
G.S. 20-217(g) Offenses committed on or after December 1, 2013	Passing a stopped school bus and striking a person, causing death (Class H felony)	G.S. 20-217(g1) [15]	3 years; G.S. 20-217(g1)					
G.S. 20-217(g) Offenses committed on or after December 1, 2013	Second conviction of passing a stopped school bus and striking a person/striking a person and causing death	G.S. 20-217(g1) [16]	Permanent; G.S. 20-217(g1)					

14. *See supra* note 12.
15. *See supra* note 10.
16. *See supra* note 10.

www.ingramcontent.com/pod-product-compliance
Lightning Source LLC
Chambersburg PA
CBHW082114210326
41599CB00033B/6696